MW00892837

palo bytes

Quick Config Examples for Firewall Engineers

Justin Worley

ISBN: 9798559405643

© 2020. All rights reserved. No part of this publication may be reproduced, distributed, or transmitted in any form or by any means, including photocopying, recording, or other electronic or mechanical methods, without the prior written permission of the publisher, except in the case of brief quotations embodied in critical reviews and certain other noncommercial uses permitted by copyright law.

Table of Contents

Preface

The purpose of this book is to provide quick and proven examples of specific configurations in the Palo Alto Networks (PAN) Next-Generation Firewall (NGFW). I aim to avoid excessively wordy explanations and instead focus on the specific points of configuration: highlight examples that might help you streamline your configuration, gain a better understanding of the topic, or inspire you to delve deeper into the technology.

This book is intended for someone with an associate-level knowledge of the following technologies and areas of expertise: PAN NGFW, routing and switching, Microsoft server administration, and the TCP/IP protocol suite

NOTE: These examples are based on integration with a Microsoft enterprise network, so all examples use Microsoft Windows Servers for the various domain services utilized. To get the most out of this book, I recommend that you have access to a lab with a Palo Alto Networks Next-Generation Firewall, including resources to run virtual servers and a means to virtualize routing and switching infrastructure (GNS3 or Eve-NG – of course, if you have physical routers and switches, great!). As for the firewall, virtual or physical will work just the same: the only difference being the configuration of interfaces.

I believe that we're all in a continual state of learning, so if you have any insights, requests, or you find some errors in the text, please feel free to contact me via email at usaf.telephony.guy@gmail.com.

I love exploring technology and learning new and exciting ways of manipulating data communications. I hope this book will spark your exploration into the NGFW technology family and that it will drive you to move beyond the boundaries of day-to-day firewall administration.

Thank you for reading my book.

Chapter 1: Device Certificates

Your Palo needs a certificate. Why? Well, let's venture down the "rabbit hole" for a minute. Cybercrime is a massive issue these days. Why is this? Well, I believe the answer lies in a couple of reasons: more people are using the Internet for business transactions, passing along their private data between one another. On the other hand, criminals see the pervasiveness of the Internet and realize there is a major opportunity to advance malicious intentions, so they have become increasingly adept at taking advantage of this new virtual world to suit their desires. Because of this increased user vulnerability, an individual must take every precaution to safeguard his or her data. If you think about it, one must be on guard against foreign states, criminals, loose associates, certain members of his or her family, and even the local government. Give me a break!

So, why did I just rant on about my thoughts on security? Well, as it turns out, the IT security industry, to ensure data integrity, confidentiality, non-repudiation, and a whole lot of other ambiguous words, have worked to secure our data and free us of our previous over-trusting ways. One of the steps taken: implement a new protocol called hypertext transfer protocol SECURE (HTTPS). I don't want to bore you with any more details you probably already know, but my point is that most Internet traffic is now tunneled inside separate transport layer security (TLS) encrypted flows. What does this mean for you, the firewall engineer? Well, when you administer your firewall through the web GUI, you want to make sure the connection is secure and cannot be captured for viewing and exploitation. On the other hand, when users access resources outside of your network, you'll want to inspect the traffic for viruses and other vulnerabilities, which to do so, will require you to decrypt that annoying TLS tunnel. This is where we finally get to the point of this chapter: configuring your Palo firewall with a certificate.

As it pertains to your situation and goals, you might only use the certificate for securing the web GUI, or, you might take it further and decrypt traffic for content inspection. It's up to you. In this chapter, I am going to provide a quick and easy way to get one certificate to meet all your needs.

PKI configuration, at its core, can be summed up in these four steps:
1. Generate a certificate signing request (CSR) on the device receiving the cert
2. Import the CSR into a certificate authority (CA) server and sign the request
3. Download the signed cert from the CA and import into the device
4. Import the CA certs (root and intermediate root) into the device trusted root store

That's it, and I'm going to make it even better. I will be changing step one and generating the certificate signing request and private key on a Windows machine within my Active Directory (AD) domain, then, once the certificate is signed and imported back into the machine to join its private key mate, I will export and import the certificate and private key into the Palo firewall.

NOTE: This does, however, introduce a potential security risk: having the private key on another system and making it exportable.

Understand that you should delete any instances of the private key except for the system where it's intended to live. For example, once you import the certificate and private key into the Palo firewall, delete any instances of this package from all other systems except the Palo. As far as the potential vulnerability, you need to weigh the risks versus the benefits in each case. For instance, if you have one firewall that needs a certificate, then the CSR option makes sense. On the other hand, if you have multiple firewalls that need a certificate, you can use the "exported" option to consolidate by including subject alternative names (SAN) for each device into one certificate and private key pair for all devices. It's up to you. Also, your configuration options are limited when using the Palo CSR method. If you use a Windows machine to generate the request, you'll have many more options available. So, with that said, let's get to it.

Section 1.1: Generate the certificate request

First, log in to any Windows machine (workstation or server), open Command Prompt, type in "certlm", and press enter. This will open Microsoft Management Console (MMC) with the snap-in "Certificates – Local Computer" already loaded.

Next, expand the "Personal" folder, select and right-click the "Certificates" subfolder, then select "All Tasks", "Advanced Operations", and "Create Custom Request…"

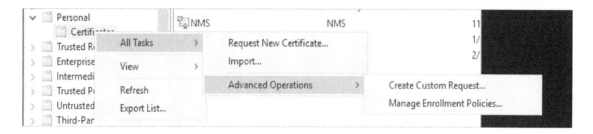

Once the dialog box opens, click "Next", then, on the next page, select "Proceed without enrollment policy" and click "Next".

Leave the Custom Request "Template" and "Request format" settings at the default values and click "Next".

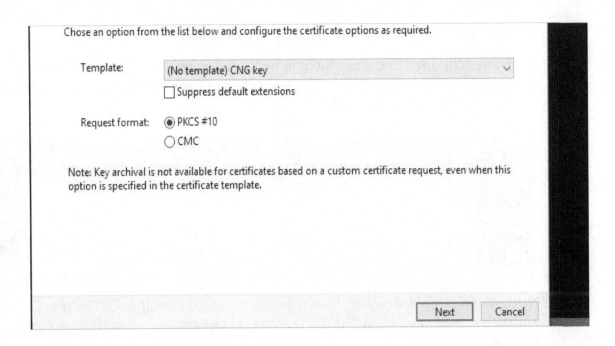

Chose an option from the list below and configure the certificate options as required.

Template: (No template) CNG key

☐ Suppress default extensions

Request format: ◉ PKCS #10
                 ○ CMC

Note: Key archival is not available for certificates based on a custom certificate request, even when this option is specified in the certificate template.

Next   Cancel

Once you reach the Certificate Enrollment screen, click the "Details" dropdown arrow and select "Properties".

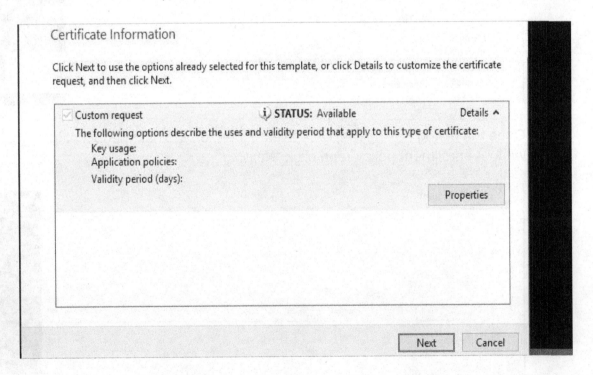

Certificate Information

Click Next to use the options already selected for this template, or click Details to customize the certificate request, and then click Next.

☑ Custom request   ⓘ STATUS: Available   Details ⌃

The following options describe the uses and validity period that apply to this type of certificate:

Key usage:
Application policies:

Validity period (days):

Properties

Next   Cancel

At this point, while accessing the "General" tab, give the certificate a "Friendly Name".

NOTE: The friendly name does not impact the validity of the certificate whatsoever.

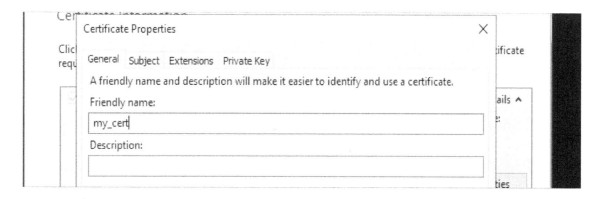

Click on the "Subject" tab, and in the "Subject name:" section, change the type to "Common name" and type in a name for the certificate. It's best to make the name something that describes the certificate's use. I used "firewall.lab.com". Even though it is not an actual URL, it will help me remember that this is a certificate meant for the firewall. Also, "Common name" is not used for verification any longer. For verification, Internet Explorer, Microsoft Edge, Google Chrome, and Mozilla Firefox all rely on subject alternative names.

Next, in the "Alternative name" section, select "DNS", and input the domain name[s] that will be used for the device[s]. Also, you can choose to input IP addresses by selecting type "IP address (v4) [(v6)]", just in case you wish to browse using the IP and you want the browser to trust it.

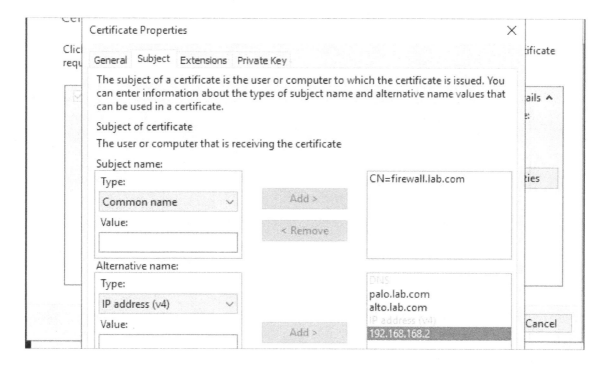

Now, skip to the "Private Key" tab at the top, click the down arrow for "Key options", change the key size to something higher than 1024, check the box for "Make private key exportable", and then click "Apply" and "OK".

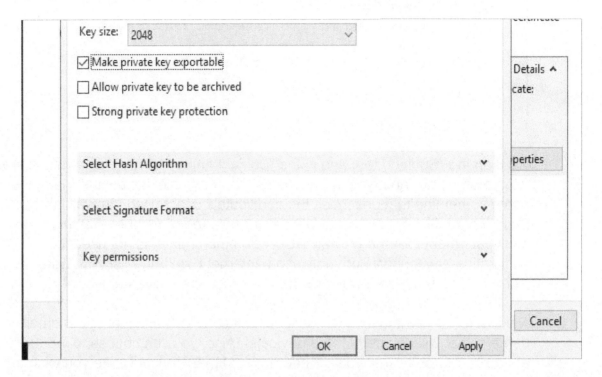

Once you're back on the "Certificate information" page, click "Next", then, identify a location to save the file and give it a name. Make sure "Base 64" is selected for file format and click "Finish".

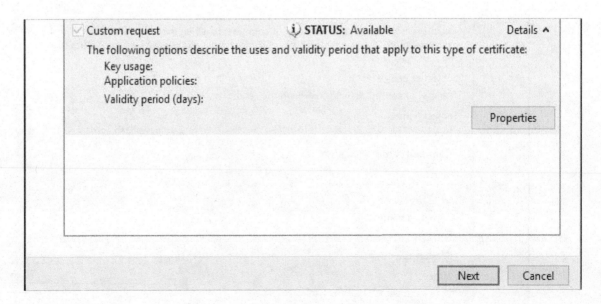

Where do you want to save the offline request?

If you want to save a copy of your certificate request or want to process the request later, save the request to your hard disk or removable media. Enter the location and name of your certificate request, and then click Finish.

File Name:

C:\Users\domain.admin\Desktop\my_request   Browse...

File format:

◉ Base 64
◯ Binary

Finish   Cancel

Section 1.2: Signing and Exporting the Certificate

Now that you have your request ready, you need to get it signed. You'll need a domain account with permission to access your CA server. Also, you'll need permission to use the "subordinate certificate authority" template. Ultimately, if your account does not have these permissions, you'll have to request assistance from an authorized administrator.

Find the certificate signing request file you saved in Step 9 of "Section 1: Generate the certificate request". In my case, I named the file "my_request". Open this file with "Notepad". It should look like this.

```
-----BEGIN NEW CERTIFICATE REQUEST-----
MIIDgjCCAmoCAQAwGzEZMBcGA1UEAwwQZmlyZXdhbGwubGFiLmNvbTCCASIwDQYJ
KoZIhvcNAQEBBQADggEPADCCAQoCggEBANE+YtY8cviUbeoIDeGuWPN3GuHzinjj
3lfyMkh5jfsvCVwMeLRrhFNGvDN9iwf6NlkrREnlbegGAqHXb13gjHTyMpYudGpn
PzwvroVrxGogJuv+f821jRqSinqXC+wAivgwTkA+sQYghUetoyeTb8ehrAgrbJsA
bMTXJSAJK6aTlECRA33nzTBUDvCKnFHz4uyboYVdJN8895yz4kKVgTw+VSBoQnda
EVYWRpjGi2RKGcpE0hXjqUqj7COkp7dYKZUIoqzJiFhV/zvooM94ggT0/nJUiO4F
/NqBru05I15L3/CJKNgzBt8h6DumUVS0Ff7IH4zC2dBCQz6YadEFQIkCAwEAAaCC
ASAwHAYKKwYBBAGCNw0CAzEOFgwxMC4wLjE4MzYzLjIIwOwYJKwYBBAGCNxUUMS4w
LAIBBQwMV0VTVC5sYWIuY29tDBBMQUJcZG9tYWluLmFkbWluDAdNTUMuRVhFMFsG
CSqGSIb3DQEJDjFOMEwwKwYDVR0RBCQwIoIMcGFsby5sYWIuY29tggxhbHRvLmxh
Yi5jb22HBMCoqAIwHQYDVR00BBYEFLiNULh7wlPbhI6Jz2Fx4pv6wa4pMGYGCisG
AQQBgjcNAgIxWDBWAgEAHk4ATQBpAGMAcgBvAHMAbwBmAHQAIABTAG8AZgB0AHcA
YQByAGUAIABLAGUAeQAgAFMAdABvAHIAYQBnAGUAIABQAHIAbwB2AGGkAZAB1AHID
AQAwDQYJKoZIhvcNAQELBQADggEBAKJF+ySTEYy8gGSe4TMSA1Q/phUGPyRRgtZB
fgptB7zpt7Gk4GcSOjFDDF9cPjANh3jWg6ViqbzTKfFROKEgiPkkwlwHG1OH0zwg
I4NYe+Tjo6VcKVBtGpyjC9GvN+SfuzX8AqYlnhdxhveK1tfIm6F+sUkTPL1tFyN6
2VSrD5ZQ7T/AsXHWYL21x7+3cdROCA558zFF4xK9QswnPJYXkIgKnH0JlMxhEUmr
uUV7v3GnJSULyAOXalZ+uhdoc86VOMD9RheOC5hC6NYg30JJp/fiOHV1CrqsP7nP
7jcSqWF/CeelSHpaoDqfrUuDOszjp90706bCUIK1wyhWAd4s5Uk=
-----END NEW CERTIFICATE REQUEST-----
```

Select and copy all the text, and then log into the web UI for your CA server (https://SERVERNAME/certsrv). Then, select "Request a certificate", select "advanced certificate request", paste the copied base64 text into the "Base-64-encoded certificate request (CMC or PKCS #10 or PKCS #7):" box, then, under the "Certificate Template", select "Subordinate Certificate Authority", and lastly click "Submit".

Saved Request:

Base-64-encoded
certificate request
(CMC or
PKCS #10 or
PKCS #7):

```
I4NYe+Tjo6VcKVBtGpyjC9GvN+SfuzX8AqYlnh
2VSrD5ZQ7T/AsXHWYL21x7+3cdROCA558zFF4x
uUV7v3GnJSULyAOXalZ+uhdoc86VOMD9RheOC5
7jcSqWF/CeelSHpaoDqfrUuDOszjp90706bCUI
-----END NEW CERTIFICATE REQUEST-----
```

Certificate Template:

Subordinate Certification Authority ▼

Additional Attributes:

Attributes:

Submit >

On the "Certificate Issued" page, select "Base 64 encoded", and click "Download certificate".

NOTE: You can download all certificates in the chain, but for the purposes of loading into the Palo, I've had negative results with this option, so I chose to import the root/intermediate root certificates separately.

Your file will save as "certnew.cer", so make a note of where it is saved.

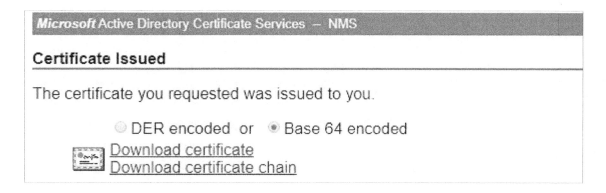

Return to the "Certificates – Local Computer" MMC snap-in, select the "Personal" folder, right-click and select "All Tasks", and then select "Import".

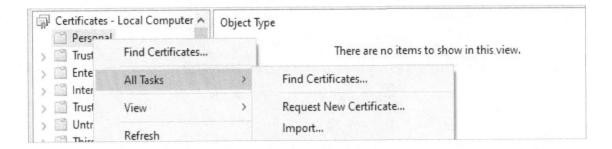

On the import wizard, "Local Machine" will be selected (grayed out). This is fine, click "Next". Locate the file you just saved (certnew.cer) and click next. Select "Place all certificates in the following store" and select "Personal", then click "Next". On the next page, click "Finish".

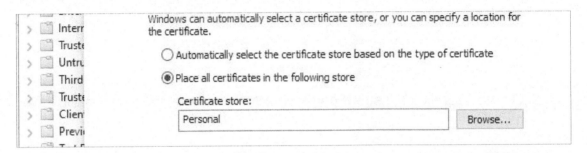

Once the import completes successfully, return to the "Certificates – Local Computer" MMC snap-in. Under the "Personal" folder, click on the "Certificates" subfolder. You should see the new certificate, "firewall.lab.com", with a "key" icon identifying this certificate has a private key.

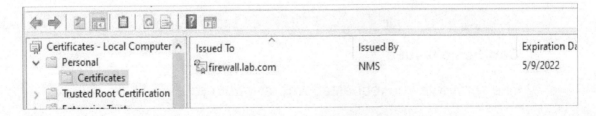

Now, it's time to export. Right-click on the certificate, select "All Tasks", and select "Export".

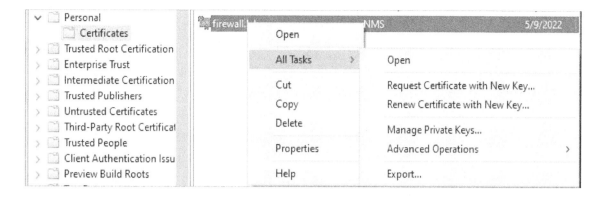

On the "Certificate Export Wizard", click "Next", select "Yes, export the private key" and click "Next", then under the "Export File Format" page, make sure "Personal Information Exchange – PKCS #12 (.PFX)" is selected with all boxes unchecked, and click "Next".

On the "Security" page, check the box for "Password", and input a password that you'll remember. You can leave "Encryption" set to the default setting. Click "Next".

Put in a file name/location to save the file, then click "Next". On the next page, click "Finish":

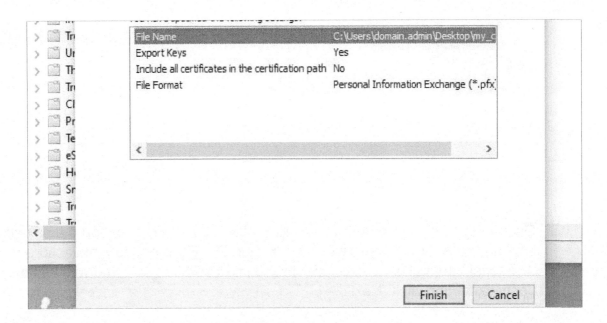

Now with the certificate and private key exported and saved to your machine, it's time to get it loaded into the Palo firewall.

Section 1.3: Importing the certificate into the Palo Firewall

In this last section, we'll be loading the exported certificate into the Palo firewall, and we'll update some settings to begin using this certificate for web UI security. Also, I will briefly cover settings that will be needed for future decryption policy use.

First, log into your Palo firewall, then click on the Device tab, in the left-hand column click on and expand the Certificate Management section, then select the Certificates link.

At the bottom of the page, click Import, select "Certificate Type – Local (radio button)", fill in the "Certificate Name" field, browse to/locate the certificate you exported in the previous section, make sure "File Format" is set to "Encrypted Private Key and Certificate (PKCS12), then enter the password you set when you exported the certificate, confirm the password, and click "OK".

Once the import completes, you'll see your new certificate listed in the store with the CA and Key boxes checked.

Now, it's time to assign this certificate as the local firewall web UI security certificate. In the left-hand column, click on and expand the Certificate

Management section, then click the SSL/TLS Service Profile link. At the bottom of the page, click Add, give the profile a name, choose the new certificate you previously imported, then set your minimum/maximum TLS protocol versions and click "OK".

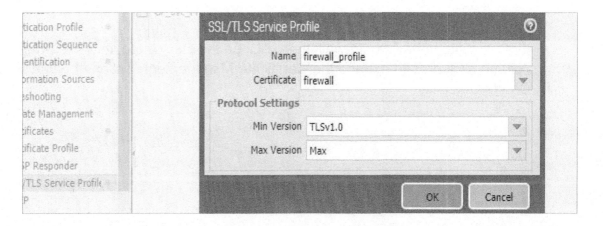

Next, in the left-hand column at the top, click the Setup link, select the "Management" tab, and click the gear icon for the "General Settings" section. Once the "General Settings" configuration page opens, set the "SSL/TLS Service Profile" to the new profile you just created, then click "OK".

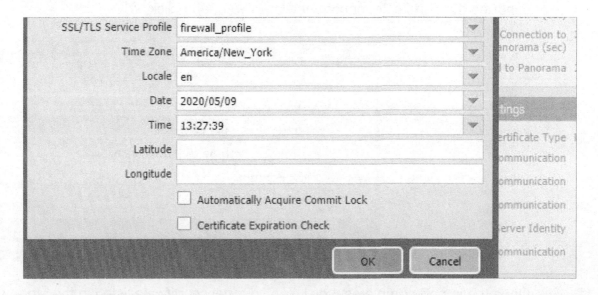

Next, click the Commit link to apply the configuration. Once it completes, refresh the browser and view the certificate by clicking the lock icon in the browser address bar, then select the link to view the certificate (this process will be different for each browser type). You will notice that it's issued to "firewall.lab.com" in my case. Then, click on the Details tab of the Certificate window and select "Subject Alternative Name". You'll see the various DNS/IP alternative names used during the certificate creation process in Section 1.

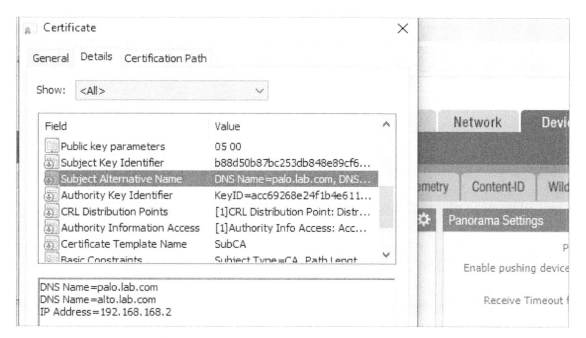

Just for fun, we can test whether the browser trusts all alternative name entries. I have a DNS type A record for "palo.lab.com", but I do not have one for "alto.lab.com". I will modify my "hosts" file to map the IP to the name manually.

NOTE: To modify your "hosts" file, open your text editor of choice using the "Run as Administrator" option, then open the file, through the editor, at "C:\Windows\System32\Drivers\etc\hosts". Lastly, make your changes and save the file. To test, you need to perform a "ping" to the domain, which will display the IP address. Name lookup will not work for host file entries since the client bypasses the "hosts" file when performing a name server lookup.

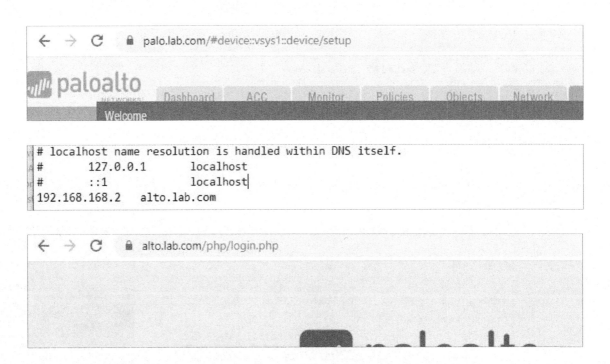

I want to wrap up this chapter with a brief discussion on using certificates for Forward Proxy Decryption. As you know, in the first section, we chose to use the subordinate certification authority template to create our certificate. The reason: the Palo firewall can use this certificate to decrypt the traffic for inspection purposes. In the basic sense, the Palo becomes a CA server and signs certificates based on information contained in the original certificate. I don't want to get into this too much right now, but just know that you have settings that must be enabled for the firewall to use a specific certificate for decryption purposes. I've provided a quick example below. Navigate to the firewall Device tab, in the left-hand column, expand the Certificate Management section and select the Certificates link, then click to open the certificate you want to use for decryption. Once the "Certificate information" box is open, you'll see some checkboxes at the bottom of the configuration page. Notice the "Forward Trust Certificate" and "Forward Untrust Certificate" checkboxes. These are the settings that will dictate which certificate is used in Forward Proxy Decryption.

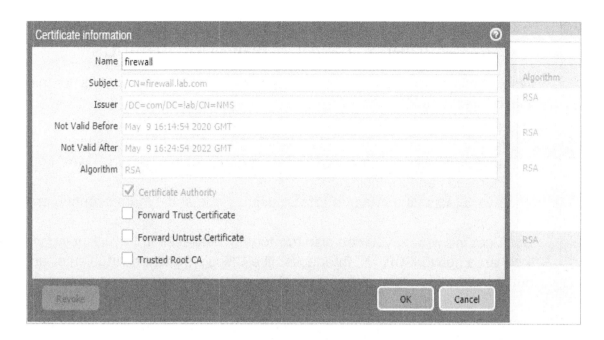

This concludes the "Device Certificates" chapter. As I stated before, your firewall needs a certificate, no questions. But I also hope you can see from the steps I laid out, that creating certificates and configuring the firewall to use these certificates is a simple process. You always want to secure web GUIs, for all devices, but also in the case of decryption, if you do not decrypt the flow, it is impossible to inspect the traffic for viruses, spyware, vulnerabilities, files…the list goes on and on. So, get with the program and decrypt. Now, once your web GUI is secure, you can safely begin to configure your firewall, and the best place to start: your Network settings.

Chapter 2: Layer 3 Network Settings

When it comes to "Network" settings, you have quite a few options contained within three main categories:

- Virtual Wire (mimics a direct physical connection between two interfaces)
- Layer2 (acts as a switch port, learning media access control (MAC) addresses and switching connections)
- Layer3 (acts as a router interface, using static and dynamic routing protocols)

Don't get me wrong, you can also run routed interfaces in Layer2 using virtual local area network "VLAN" interfaces, like Cisco's switched virtual interface (SVI), but to keep this simple, just know that Layer2 is for switching and Layer3 is for routing. These three options alone provide a great deal of flexibility in configuration. In addition, you need to create zones for the specific interface types you create, and if using Layer3, you must also configure a virtual router to allow routing between the various interfaces.

This chapter will walk through the process of configuring a new Layer3 interface and associated zone, and we'll then configure a virtual router to enable routing between two interfaces, then we'll finish up with configuring an additional type of Layer3 interface: the Subinterface.

Just to give you an overview of what we'll be doing, I have created a couple of diagrams showing my planned topology. In this first diagram, you can see the design is simple. There is a client zone named "Guest" that will hold my test client (1.1.1.2/24), and 1.1.1.1/24 will be the gateway interface on the firewall. All default traffic from this client will cross the firewall into the "Outside" zone to reach the Internet via my commercial ISP router at 10.0.0.1/24.

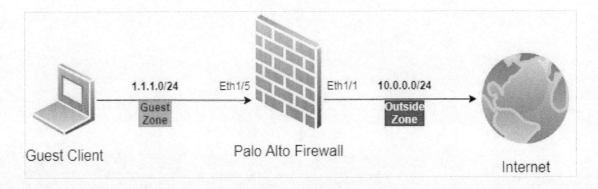

To give you a sense of what is really taking place, I have created another diagram below. It takes a decent amount of internal routing to make this work. As I said before, you must configure a virtual router for a Layer3 configuration. I currently have a virtual router named "VR". For me to provide an example of a virtual router configuration, I will be creating a new virtual router named "Guest", and I will configure routing between the two virtual routers within the firewall. This is like running virtual routing and forwarding (VRF), except unlike Cisco, Palo provides an option to interconnect separate tables internally. Here's a more detailed version of what's taking place.

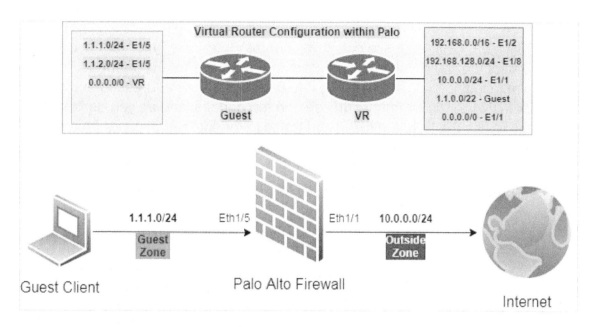

As you can see, the "Guest" virtual router knows of two routes, which will egress through the E1/5 interface and one default route that will forward to the "VR" virtual router.

- 1.1.1.0/24 – Guest – E1/5 (Connected)
- 1.1.2.0/24 – Guest2 – (*will be used for sub-interface example*)
- 0.0.0.0/0 – Default – (Next Hop VR)

On the VR side, VR knows four local routes and a default route.

- 192.168.0.0/16 – Internal Network – E1/2 (Next Hop 192.168.255.2)
- 192.168.128.0/24 – Server Farm – E1/8 (Connected)
- 10.0.0.0/24 – Network between Outside interface and ISP router – E1/1 (Connected)
- 0.0.0.0/0 – Default – E1/1 (Next Hop 10.0.0.1)
- 1.1.0.0/22 – Guest Network – "Guest" virtual router

Alright, now that you have an idea of the topology, let's get configuring.

Section 2.1: Configuring the Layer3 Interfaces and Zones

Go to the firewall Network tab, select the Interfaces link in the left-hand column, and choose an interface to configure. In my example, I am going to use "ethernet1/5".

Click on the interface to configure, set the "Interface Type" to "Layer3", then select the "IPv4" tab and configure an IP address for the interface. In my case, I'm using 1.1.1.1/24, but it's best to use a private IP address to avoid conflicts with live public internet addresses. In the end, as long as you don't try to advertise the IP to the ISP, send traffic to the Internet sourced from an active public IP, or run into an issue of needing to access an Internet resource that is using the same address, there shouldn't be an issue. Also, you may choose to input the IP/mask directly, or you can create an address object instead. It's up to you. Once you are finished, click "OK" to close the Ethernet Interface configuration page.

NOTE: When you assign the IP, be sure to identify the subnet mask in CIDR notation. If you only list the IP address, the firewall will read it as a /32 mask. It's an ethernet segment, so we need to identify the full range of IPs and establish network and broadcast addresses for proper switching of broadcast and unknown unicast traffic.

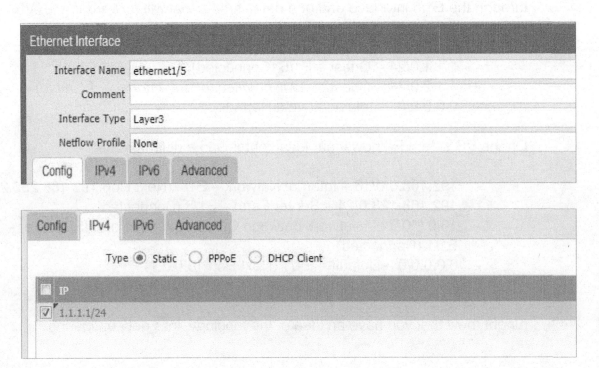

Next, click on the Zones link in the left-hand column and click the Add link at the bottom of the page. Give your new zone a name (in my case, I'm naming it "Guest"), set the "Type" to "Layer3", then in the "Interfaces" box, click "Add" at the bottom of the box and select the new Layer3 Interface you previously configured. Once you're finished, click "OK" to close the Zone configuration page.

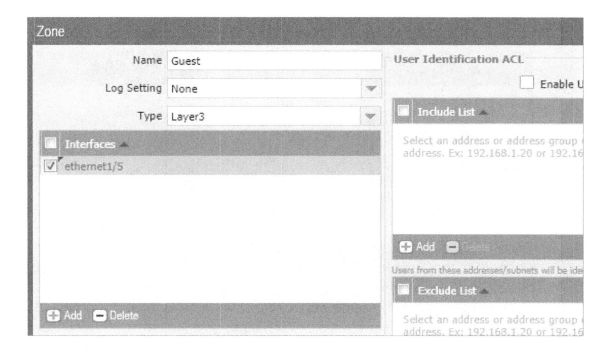

Section 2.2: Configuring A Virtual Router

Now, the last thing we need to do for routing is to configure the virtual router. Click on the Virtual Routers link in the left-hand column and click Add at the bottom of the screen. Give your virtual router a name (in my case, I'm going to use "Guest"). Next, with the "General" tab selected, click "Add", and select the interface you previously configured.

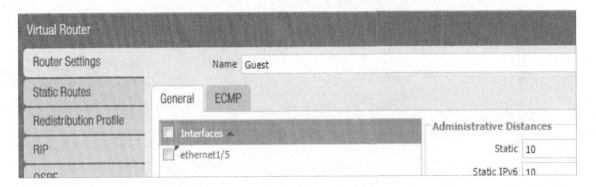

Once finished, click on the "Static Routes" tab on the left-hand side. Then, click on "Add" at the bottom of the configuration page. We're only going to create a default route to the other virtual router (VR). Since we identified the subnet mask for the interface (E1/5), we do not need a route for this directly connected network (1.1.1.0/24). Now, for the "VR" route, give it a name (in my case, I'm naming it "Default"), then set the Destination to "0.0.0.0/0", set Interface to "None", change Next Hop to "Next VR", select the virtual router in the dropdown box below the Next Hop dropdown box (in my case "VR"), adjust the Admin Distance and Metric if you wish, and make sure the Route Table setting is set to "Unicast", then click "OK".

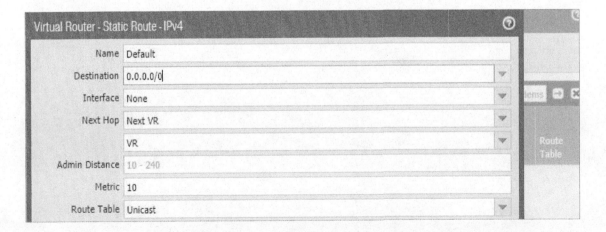

Once you return to the main "Virtual Router" configuration page, click "OK" to close the page, then finish it off with a Commit. Once the commit is complete, select the Virtual Routers link in the left-hand column, and with the virtual routers listed in the main page, click on the "More Runtime Stats" link on the right-hand side.

Name	Interfaces	Configuration	Runtime Stats
Guest	ethernet1/5	Static Routes: 1 ECMP status: Disabled	More Runtime Stats

Once it opens, you are presented with the information contained in the "Route Table" tab. Like cisco express forwarding (CEF), you also have the option to view the hardware-based "Forwarding Table" simply by selecting the tab "Forwarding Table".

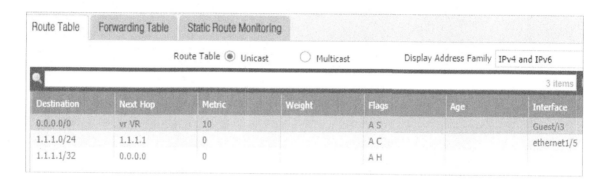

Route Table | Forwarding Table | Static Route Monitoring

Route Table ⦿ Unicast   ◯ Multicast   Display Address Family IPv4 and IPv6

3 items

Destination	Next Hop	Metric	Weight	Flags	Age	Interface
0.0.0.0/0	vr VR	10		A S		Guest/i3
1.1.1.0/24	1.1.1.1	0		A C		ethernet1/5
1.1.1.1/32	0.0.0.0	0		A H		

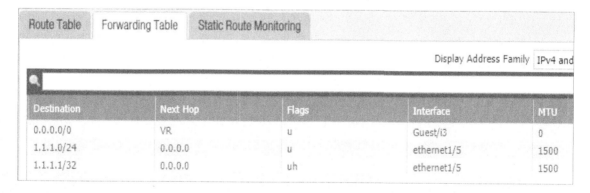

Route Table | Forwarding Table | Static Route Monitoring

Display Address Family IPv4 and

Destination	Next Hop	Flags	Interface	MTU
0.0.0.0/0	VR	u	Guest/i3	0
1.1.1.0/24	0.0.0.0	u	ethernet1/5	1500
1.1.1.1/32	0.0.0.0	uh	ethernet1/5	1500

There is a legend at the bottom of each page to tell you what the flags mean, but I'll briefly describe what you're seeing in the examples above. For the "Route Table" page, "A" means "active", "S" means "static", "C" means "connected", and "H" means "host". So, there are three active routes: a static route, a directly connected route, and a host route.

For the "Forwarding Table", "u" means "up", and "h" means "host". So, there are three "up" adjacencies, one of which is a "host".

It's very interesting to notice that for the "VR" adjacency, the maximum transmission unit (MTU) is "0". Since it is not directed through a physical interface, there is no need to set the MTU, but once it reaches the egress port at the other virtual router, it will have to conform to the MTU, which is 1500 bytes by default for all ethernet interfaces.

Now, we need to add a route in the other virtual router "VR" to point the 1.1.1.0/24 traffic back towards the "Guest" virtual router. I am going to add in a summary route since I plan to configure another interface. The summary will be 1.1.0.0/22. This will give me four /24s 1.1.0.0/24, 1.1.1.0/24, 1.1.2.0/24, 1.1.3.0/24, although you can chop them up however you like. I'll then follow this up with a Commit and prepare to test passing traffic.

Next, configure a new client on "Guest" to use for generating traffic. I'm using a Windows 10 machine with IP address 1.1.1.2/24. For your client system, you can use whatever you like: Linux, Windows, a router, whatever, just as long as you can configure it with an IP address. Once you're configured and connected, generate a ping from the client to the gateway address on the firewall (1.1.1.1). You will not get a response.

```
C:\Users\domain.admin>ping 1.1.1.1 -w 500

Pinging 1.1.1.1 with 32 bytes of data:
Request timed out.
Request timed out.
Request timed out.
Request timed out.

Ping statistics for 1.1.1.1:
    Packets: Sent = 4, Received = 0, Lost = 4 (100% loss),
```

You can fix this by adding an "Interface Management" network profile. Under the main Network tab, In the left-hand column, click to expand the Network Profiles section, then click the "Interface Mgmt" link. Click Add at the bottom of the page. Once the Interface Management Profile configuration page pops up, give the profile a name, and under the "Network Services" section, check the box for "ping" to allow echo replies, and click "OK".

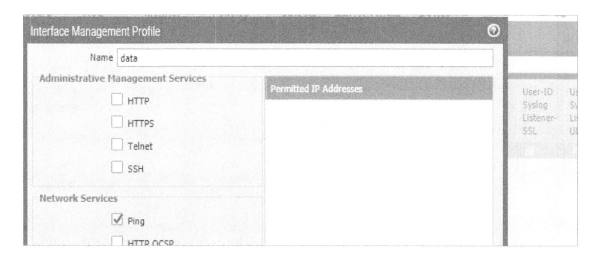

Next, in the left-hand column, click the Interfaces link, then click on and open the interface configuration page for the interface you configured previously (in my case, E1/5). Next, click the "Advanced" tab, and in the "Management Profile" dropdown box, click to add the new "Interface Mgmt" profile you just created.

Lastly, click "OK" and perform a Commit. Once that completes, go back to your "Guest" client and perform another ping. You should get a response this time.

```
C:\Users\domain.admin>ping 1.1.1.1 -w 500

Pinging 1.1.1.1 with 32 bytes of data:
Reply from 1.1.1.1: bytes=32 time=1ms TTL=64
Reply from 1.1.1.1: bytes=32 time=1ms TTL=64
Reply from 1.1.1.1: bytes=32 time=1ms TTL=64
Reply from 1.1.1.1: bytes=32 time=1ms TTL=64

Ping statistics for 1.1.1.1:
    Packets: Sent = 4, Received = 4, Lost = 0 (0% loss),
Approximate round trip times in milli-seconds:
    Minimum = 1ms, Maximum = 1ms, Average = 1ms
```

To complete this section, we need to see the traffic pass. For this to happen, we'll need to set up a simple security policy to allow the traffic to traverse the firewall and connect with a resource. I am going to allow traffic from the "Guest" zone into my "Farm" zone so that I can establish a connection with DNS and a local webserver. So, on the main page, click the Policies tab at the top. In the left-hand column, select the Security link, highlight the first rule, and click Add at the bottom of the page. Give your policy a name (in my case, I'm using "Guest-to-Farm").

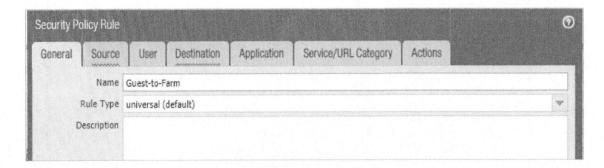

Next, select the "Source" tab, and in the "Source Zone" configuration box, click "Add" and select the "Guest" zone.

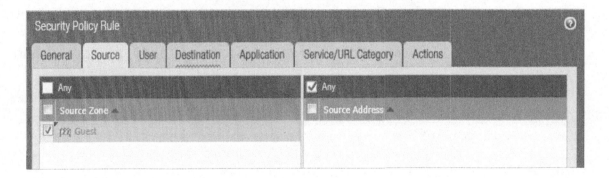

Then, select the "Destination" tab and add in the destination zone you're trying to reach (in my case, I'm using the "Farm" zone).

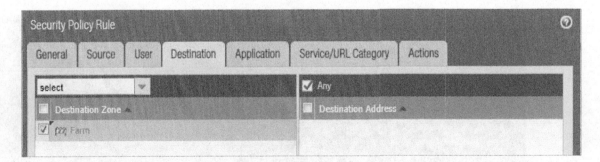

That should be all you need for this quick test. Click "OK" at the bottom of the "Security Policy Rule" configuration page to close it out and perform a Commit. Next, from your Guest client, try to access a resource in the zone you chose for the previous step. For me, I'm going to perform a name lookup for "web.lab.com", which will query my DNS server in the "Farm" zone, then, I will browse to this site, which is also in my "Farm" zone.

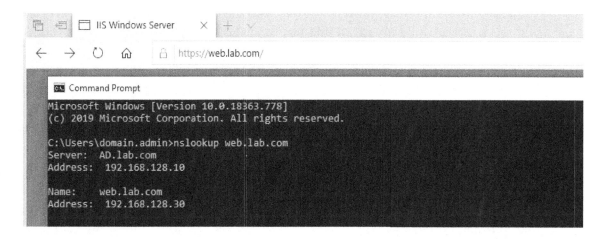

As you can see from the background browser page and my Command Prompt name server lookup, both were successful.

Lastly, go into the firewall, select the Monitor tab at the top, click on the Traffic link in the left-hand column, and add filter "(addr.src eq 1.1.1.2) and (app eq dns)" in the log search bar. Then, select the URL Filtering link in the left-hand column, and add filter "(addr.src in 1.1.1.2) and (url contains web.lab.com)".

NOTE: My chosen URL is only an example. Please use whatever URL you used for your browsing test. You should see the traffic.

And that is it. You now have a new working Layer3 interface and zone, with routing configured, and a security policy allowing the traffic so you can verify. Now, we're going to wrap up this chapter with one more topic: Subinterfaces.

Section 2.3: Configuring a Subinterface

Subinterfaces allow you to take one physical Layer3 interface and divide it up logically into multiple interfaces. If you have any experience with Cisco routers, I'm sure you're fully aware of this configuration. The great thing: Palo does it pretty much the same way.

On the topic of 802.1q (VLAN tagging), you need to understand a couple of principles: dot1q, as it's called, functions based on inserting tags in the Layer2 header of a frame so that it can identify the VLAN that the packet is associated with as it passes between layer2 devices over a VLAN trunk. There is always a "native" VLAN, meaning a VLAN that sends traffic over the trunk untagged, and all other "allowed" VLANs shall use a tag (although, at least in the case of Cisco, you can specify that the native VLAN needs to be tagged). Just for reference, I did a quick configuration and performed a packet capture to show you what a dot1q tag looks like.

```
∨ Ethernet II, Src: VMware_a3:37:e7 (00:50:56:a3:37:e7), Dst: PaloAlto_83:bc:14 (08:30:6b:83:bc:14)
   > Destination: PaloAlto_83:bc:14 (08:30:6b:83:bc:14)
   > Source: VMware_a3:37:e7 (00:50:56:a3:37:e7)
     Type: 802.1Q Virtual LAN (0x8100)
∨ 802.1Q Virtual LAN, PRI: 0, DEI: 0, ID: 2001
     000. .... .... .... = Priority: Best Effort (default) (0)
     ...0 .... .... .... = DEI: Ineligible
     .... 0111 1101 0001 = ID: 2001
     Type: IPv4 (0x0800)
```

As you can see, the EtherType immediately following the source MAC address is 0x8100, which identifies that a dot1q tag will follow. Normally, this would show 0x0800, identifying the next header as IPv4 (0x86dd for IPv6). After the first ethertype field, the dot1q tag gets added, then it is followed up with another ethertype field to identify the next header: in this case, IPv4. The dot1q header provides 3 bits for priority (often referred to as Class of Service (CoS)), 1 bit for discard eligible/ineligible, and 12 bits to identify the VLAN (0-4095), which in this case is Vlan 2001.

Alright, it's time to configure a Subinterface.

Click on the Network tab at the top, highlight the interface you previously configured in this chapter, and click the Add Subinterface link at the bottom of the page. Once the "Layer3 Subinteface" configuration page opens, add a subinterface number (in my case, I used "2001" to match the VLAN tag), add the VLAN number to the "Tag" form field, and select "Guest" for both the "Virtual Router" and "Security Zone" dropdown boxes.

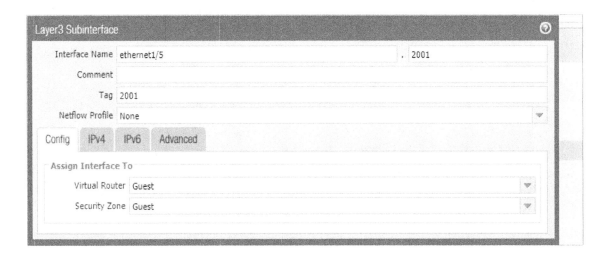

Next, select the "IPv4" tab, and input the IP address you wish to use with a "CIDR notation" subnet mask added (in my case, based on the summary route (1.1.0.0/22) I used in the virtual router configuration earlier, I have chosen to use 1.1.2.1/24).

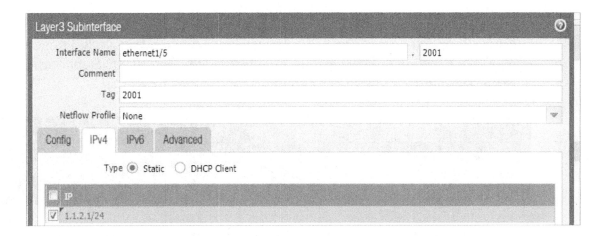

Lastly, click on the "Advanced" tab and select a "Management Profile" in the "Other Info" section using the dropdown box (in my case, I'm using Management Profile "data", which I previously configured for the first interface).

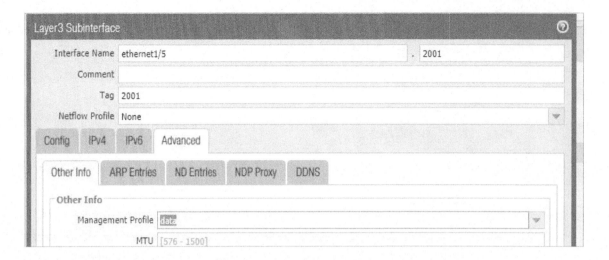

Once you're finished with these settings, click "OK" at the bottom of the "Layer3 Subinterface" configuration page, and then Commit the config.

So, at this point, we have two broadcast domains on the same interface (1.1.1.0/24, and 1.1.2.0/24), which are separated using dot1q tagging (untagged for 1.1.1.0/24 and tagged with 2001 for 1.1.2.0/24). For my topology, the E1/5 interface connects to a Cisco 3560-8pc switch. To make this work, I need to configure a trunk on the switch side to differentiate each VLAN/Subnet/Broadcast domain. Here is a snapshot of my config.

```
interface FastEthernet0/3
 switchport trunk encapsulation dot1q
 switchport trunk native vlan 2000
 switchport trunk allowed vlan 2000,2001
 switchport mode trunk
end
```

I have the native VLAN set to 2000, which supports my 1.1.1.0/24 subnet from the primary E1/5 interface (untagged) on the Palo. For the new subnet (1.1.2.0/24), I am tagging with a VLAN of 2001, so I have allowed that VLAN over the trunk. Also, you'll notice that I have allowed the native VLAN. It is possible to set a native VLAN and not allow it over the trunk. In addition, I have a trunked connection to a hypervisor (ESXi) so I can receive tagged traffic and assign it to various virtual machines.

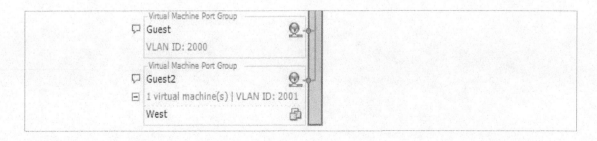

Lastly, I update my virtual machine "Network Adapter" settings to the new "Port Group", and I'm then ready to change my client IP and connect.

Now, if you do not have a dot1q capable switch or a system that is capable of handling tags, I have another option for you. You can make your subinterface "Untagged".

In the Palo, under the Network tab, highlight the subinterface you just created, and click Delete at the bottom of the page. Then, click on the Interface (in my case, ethernet1/5) to open the "Ethernet Interface" configuration page, select the "Advanced" tab, and check the box at the bottom for "Untagged Subinterface". Then, click "OK".

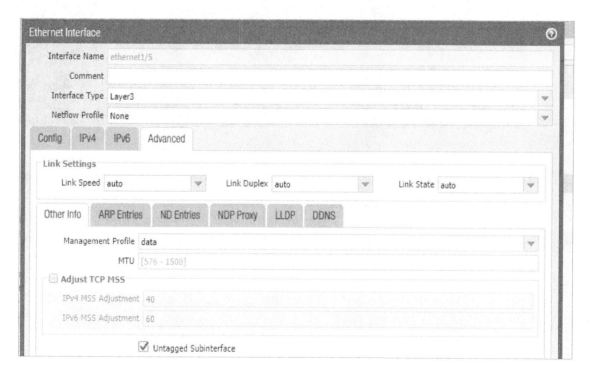

Next, highlight the interface (ethernet1/5), and click "Add Subinterface" at the bottom of the screen. Follow the same procedures in steps 1 – 3 but leave the "Tag" form field blank. Once you're finished, click "OK" and Commit the config.

In a sense, you've just configured a secondary address for the same layer2 segment. What this means: traffic for the 1.1.1.0/24 network and 1.1.2.0/24 network will be present on the same layer2 network. For your client, you can assign it an IP address in either subnet. If you use the proper gateway address, you'll be able to connect to outside resources.

```
Ethernet adapter Ethernet:

   Connection-specific DNS Suffix  . :
   IPv4 Address. . . . . . . . . . . : 1.1.1.2
   Subnet Mask . . . . . . . . . . . : 255.255.255.0
   Default Gateway . . . . . . . . . : 1.1.1.1

C:\Users\domain.admin>ping 192.168.128.10

Pinging 192.168.128.10 with 32 bytes of data:
Reply from 192.168.128.10: bytes=32 time=1ms TTL=127
Reply from 192.168.128.10: bytes=32 time=1ms TTL=127
Reply from 192.168.128.10: bytes=32 time=1ms TTL=127
Reply from 192.168.128.10: bytes=32 time=1ms TTL=127
```

```
Ethernet adapter Ethernet:

   Connection-specific DNS Suffix  . :
   IPv4 Address. . . . . . . . . . . : 1.1.2.2
   Subnet Mask . . . . . . . . . . . : 255.255.255.0
   Default Gateway . . . . . . . . . : 1.1.2.1

C:\Users\domain.admin>ping 192.168.128.10

Pinging 192.168.128.10 with 32 bytes of data:
Reply from 192.168.128.10: bytes=32 time=1ms TTL=127
Reply from 192.168.128.10: bytes=32 time=1ms TTL=127
Reply from 192.168.128.10: bytes=32 time=1ms TTL=127
Reply from 192.168.128.10: bytes=32 time=1ms TTL=127
```

So, as you can see, you have a great deal of flexibility when it comes to configuring Layer3 interfaces and associated routing. In this chapter, I used static routing. I did not get into configuring routing protocols, but just so you know, the Palo can run routing information protocol (RIP), open shortest path first (OSPFv2 and v3), and border gateway protocol (BGP). I encourage you to lab these up and have fun.

Now that the interfaces and routing are configured, we need to reach the Internet, so where's my NAT???

Chapter 3: Network Address Translation

Network Address Translation, or "NAT" for short, allows you to manipulate the following IP and TCP/UDP header information.

NOTE: TCP/UDP header checksum gets recalculated based on pseudo IP header change

- Source IP
- Destination IP
- Source TCP/UDP Port
- Destination TCP/UDP Port

Now, why would you want to manipulate these header fields? Well, on the surface, NAT fixes a glaring problem that we face: enabling the use of private IP address space (RFC 1918) to extend the life of IPv4, while at the same time allowing everyone to connect to public Internet resources. To expand on that description further, the IEEE designated ranges of IP addresses to be used in private networks.

- 10.0.0.0/8
- 172.16.0.0/12
- 192.168.0.0/16

These ranges are never to be advertised into, or routable over, the public Internet. This allows multiple users to utilize the same IP address ranges without ever experiencing address conflicts, while at the same time conserving the publicly routable IPv4 address space to prolong the life of global IPv4. However, when using the private IP address space, how do you successfully connect to a public Internet resource when Internet resources have no way of knowing how to route traffic back to you? The answer is NAT. If you have 1000 clients on your internal network using a private IP address space (say, 192.168.0.0/22, ranging from 192.168.0.0 to 192.168.3.255), and you have one publicly routable IP address you've purchased from the ISP (example: 1.1.1.1), you can use NAT for outbound traffic and differentiate each flow using TCP and UDP ports: 65536 ports each.

NOTE: You can also use static NAT in a "one IP for one IP" match, but it's not nearly as efficient.

For the NAT operation I described above, how would this affect the flow listed below:

- 192.168.0.1 source TCP-50000 is connecting to 172.217.0.1 destination TCP-443

Once this flow hits the boundary NAT device (firewall), the NAT device, via a configured policy, will rewrite the source address as the public-facing IP address (1.1.1.1), and to keep flows separate and distinguishable, it will use a range of TCP and UDP ports (say 1024 - 65535) to rewrite the source port.

- 1.1.1.1 source TCP-1024 is connecting to 172.217.0.1 destination TCP-443

In this case, 172.217.0.1 will know how to return traffic the client because it can route to the public IP address (1.1.1.1), and since NAT devices maintain stateful NAT tables (remembers the inside local to inside global mapping – IP and port), traffic can successfully return to the client. This configuration I just described is known as one form of "Source NAT". You might also hear it described as "Port Address Translation" or "NAT overload", both of which are well-known and valid references to the technique. Source NAT solves the problem of clients being able to request connections to public Internet resources, but what about the public Internet requesting connections to your internal network resources, say your public-facing web server?

"Destination NAT" enables Internet resources to initiate connections and connect to your internal resources. For instance, let's reverse the Source NAT example I provided earlier.

- 172.217.0.1 source TCP-50000 is connecting to 1.1.1.1 destination TCP-443

For the sake of argument, let's say your web server is "web.lab.com" with a private IP address of 192.168.0.1. Your public DNS "A" record tells the Internet that web.lab.com is reachable via 1.1.1.1. This gets the traffic to your firewall's outside interface, but you need to change the destination IP to 192.168.0.1 for the flow to connect to the webserver. In this case, we end up with a rewrite of:

- 172.217.0.1 source TCP-50000 is connecting to 192.168.0.1 destination TCP-443

There is no need to rewrite the source ephemeral port, and we need to maintain the destination port since the server is listening for traffic on that port. Now, I'd like to mention that if you had multiple web servers, and you wanted them to be reachable via the Internet, you could add NAT policies with different destination ports (say 1.1.1.1 TCP-443 to reach web.lab.com (192.168.0.1), and 1.1.1.1 TCP

8443 to reach intranet.lab.com (192.168.1.1). This technique is commonly known as "Port Forwarding". If you have the luxury of owning a range of public IP addresses, then you'll have fewer issues with trying to engineer differentiation. However, unless you're a medium to large business, you're probably relying on one public IP address. I'll use my home lab as an example: I have one dynamic host configuration protocol (DHCP)-assigned public IP address from my ISP, and I use an internal dynamic DNS client to beacon out and keep a specific public "A" record updated: in case my IP address changes. By having this updated record, I am always able to connect to my public IP address. Then, I have configured port forwarding, in my ISP router, for TCP-443 which gets forwarded to my firewall outside interface. I use TCP-443 for my SSL virtual private network (VPN) connection. So, if I wanted to host a web server, I'd have to choose a different port than TCP-443 for my SSL/TLS connection inbound since I've already allocated TCP-443 to another service. I hope that better clarifies the situation. In short, you must make sure that you can differentiate the resources using IP and/or TCP/UDP port differentiation.

Lastly, you might find yourself in a situation where your DNS "A" record for an internal resource maps to the public IP, but your internal users need to connect to the inside private IP address. This situation is remedied by a technique called "U-Turn NAT". The firewall will match internal connections to the public IP, at which time it will rewrite the destination public IP address to the true internal private IP address. In these situations, you can easily maintain an internal "A" record and resolve to the private IP address, while at the same time using an external "A" record for resolving to the public IP address. This does, however, require you to maintain an internal DNS server, so that's something to consider. U-turn NAT might be a better option for you in this case. Anyway, with NAT being the obscure topic that it tends to be, I felt it necessary for the lengthy explanations. Please forgive me. Now, it's time to configure some NAT.

Section 3.1: Source NAT

First, we're going to allow our "Guest" client to reach the Internet, but before we do…

NOTE: If you are directly connected to a public IP with no additional NAT (no ISP router performing NAT), I would advise you not to allow any traffic outbound from clients using a source address that is publicly routable and not your own. In my case, I have configured my client to use 1.1.2.1. Who owns this address? A quick search via https://www.ultratools.com/tools/ipWhoisLookupRequest reveals the owner:

```
            Source: whois.apnic.net
        IP Address: 1.1.2.2

% [whois.apnic.net]
% Whois data copyright terms     http://www.apnic.net/db/dbcopyright.html

% Information related to '1.1.2.0 - 1.1.3.255'

% Abuse contact for '1.1.2.0 - 1.1.3.255' is 'anti-spam@ns.chinanet.cn.net'

inetnum:        1.1.2.0 - 1.1.3.255
netname:        CHINANET-FJ
descr:          CHINANET FUJIAN PROVINCE NETWORK
descr:          China Telecom
```

China Telecom is the owner. If I were using this address, and I didn't have an additional NAT device in place before the internal network/ISP demarcation, I would essentially be performing a source IP spoof and the traffic would never return to me, but would instead be directed to China Telecom's network. This could be considered a malicious act. If I were to generate a mass of connection requests, and all responses returned to a China Telecom resource (a server), it could be construed as a denial of service (DoS) attack.

In most cases, for your home lab, you'll have an ISP router performing NAT, and your Palo outside connection will be using a private IP address internal to your ISP router. Just understand that packets from your network, sourced with an outside public IP address with no source NAT to correct the error, have the potential to disrupt services for valid customers on the Internet. You might expect ISPs/service providers to catch and block this traffic using various techniques, such as unicast reverse path forward (uRPF), but there is no 100% guarantee that this will happen.

According to the "Mutually Agreed Norms for Routing Security" (MANRS), they describe source IP address spoofing as "…the practice of originating IP datagrams with source addresses other than those assigned to the host of origin. In simple terms, the host pretends to be some other host. This can be exploited in various ways, most notably to execute Denial of Service (DoS) reflection-amplification attacks that cause a reflector host to send traffic to the spoofed address". MANRS also describes a bias throughout the industry, "…Most equipment vendors support ingress filtering in some form. Since 2005, deployment of anti-spoofing techniques has not been a limitation of the equipment performance. It has been a limitation of desire and willingness to deploy and maintain the anti-spoofing configuration…ingress filtering is definitely not sufficiently deployed. Unfortunately, there are no benefits to a Service provider (SP) that deploys ingress filtering. There is also a widely held belief that ingress filtering only helps when it is universally deployed" (MANRS: https://www.manrs.org/isps/guide/antispoofing/).

So, in short, don't expect your ISP to stop this traffic, but be a responsible and trustworthy user, and avoid sending out Internet-based traffic sourced from IP addresses that you do not own. Alright, enough with the disclaimer, let's get configuring.

First, update the security policy to allow the traffic through. Just use the policy you created in **"Chapter 2 – Layer 3 Network Settings: Section 2 – Configuring a Virtual Router, Step 9"**. Change the policy name to "Guest-Out", then click on the "Destination" tab and add your outside zone (in my case "Outside") as a destination zone in the policy, and finally in preparation for future configurations, click on the "Service/URL Category" tab and change the "Service" dropdown box from "application-default" to "any". Click "OK" and Commit the config.

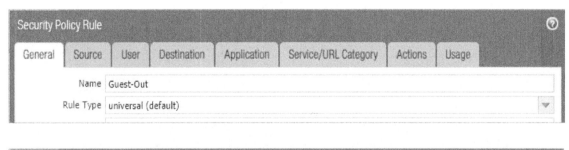

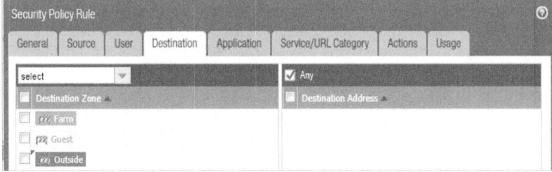

41

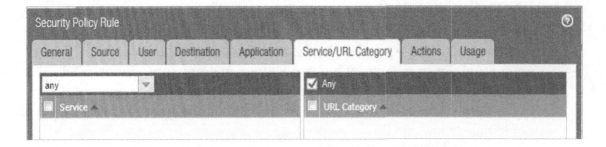

So, at this point, the traffic from your "Guest" zone to the outside zone (Internet-facing zone, in my case "Outside") can pass. In my configuration, my ISP router is performing NAT too, so since it does not have a route on the internal network to 1.1.2.2 for the return traffic, the connection is unable to complete. If I were to add a route in my ISP router saying: 1.1.0.0/22 next-hop 10.0.0.201 (Palo Outside Layer3 Interface IP address), the traffic would successfully connect bidirectionally. I do not, however, have this route in my ISP router, and besides, I want to perform NAT in the Palo firewall, so this route is unnecessary.

Next, we need to configure a Source NAT policy to allow our client to connect to Internet resources. Select the Policies tab at the top, select the NAT link in the left-hand column, and then click Add at the bottom on the page. Give the policy a name (in my case, I'm using "Guest-Internet").

Next, click on the "Original Packet" tab, select your source zone (in my case, "Guest"), select the destination zone (in my case, "Outside"), and leave the "Source Address" and "Destination Address" blocks set to "Any" (checkbox selected). Basically, in the initial stages of packet processing (slow path), the firewall will determine, via the routing tables, the source and destination zones that are associated with the flow (say 1.1.2.2 (Guest) to 8.8.8.8 (Outside – based on the default route)).

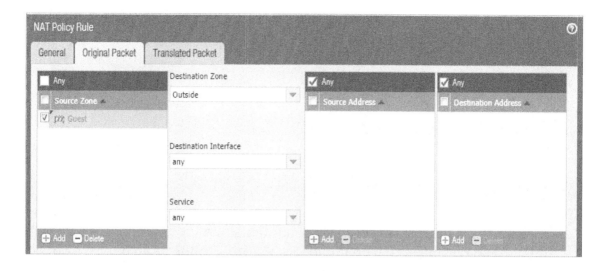

Lastly, click on the "Translated Packet" tab, in the "Source Address Translation" section, select "Dynamic IP And Port" from the "Translation Type" dropdown box, select "Translated Address" from the "Address Type" dropdown box, and click "Add" to input an IP address that is within the subnet of the configured outside interface IP address (in my case, 10.0.0.201/24 is my outside interface IP address, so I am going to use 10.0.0.202). This new IP, without a CIDR subnet mask, is parsed by the firewall as a /32 address. This is fine. The firewall, per routing, knows the default route next hop is 10.0.0.1, and it has a physical interface that resides within that subnet. Since this new address also resides within the 10.0.0.0/24 range, it will still work. Just note that when you configure a physical interface, you need a proper subnet mask in CIDR notation. Once finished configuring, click "OK" to close the configuration page and then Commit the config.

Now, from your "Guest" client, try and browse to https://httpvshttps.com (45.33.7.16). I chose this website to make it easy to track in the logs, but just in case, perform a name server lookup of the domain name to make sure the IP is still the same as previously noted. Also, feel free to use whatever Internet website you wish, just make sure to perform a name lookup so that you can grab the IP address for log filtering. With the new NAT policy in place, you should get a successful connection.

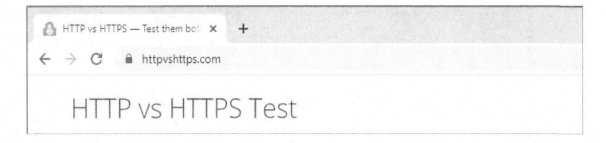

Next, in the firewall, select the Monitor tab at the top, select the Traffic link in the left-hand column, and type the following filter into the search form field: updated with your source and destination IPs.

- (addr.src in 1.1.2.2) and (addr.dst in 45.33.7.16)

Once the logs populate, click on the Details icon to open the "Detailed Log View" page. You'll see, in the "Source" section, that the "NAT IP" is 10.0.0.202, and you'll also notice that the "NAT Port" is different from the "Port" (original port). This is characteristic of Source NAT using the "Dynamic IP and Port" option. You have two other options available for "Translation Type": Dynamic IP and Static IP. These are pretty much self-explanatory, but you should know that to avoid conflicts in NAT operation when many internal clients are using it, you should always choose "Dynamic IP and Port".

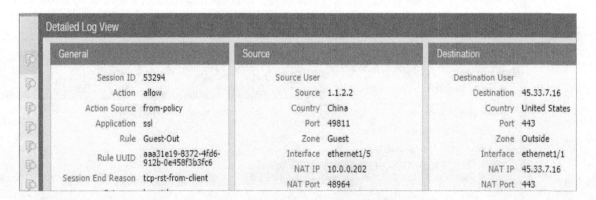

Alright, so our client can connect to outside resources, but we have a web server on the inside that needs to be reachable from the Internet, so we need to convert that public IP to a private IP.

Section 3.2: Destination NAT

In this scenario, we're going to pretend that the "Guest" client is an Internet host that needs to access https://web.lab.com. Our client resolves this domain to IP address 1.1.2.1, but the actual web server IP address is 192.168.128.30. So, we need to update the destination IP address at the firewall to form a full end-to-end connection. Select the Policies tab at the top of the page. Next, select the NAT link in the left-hand column, and click Add at the bottom of the screen. Once the "NAT Policy Rule" page comes up, add a name (in my case, I'll be using "Guest-to-WebServer").

NOTE: When you configure a destination NAT policy, consider the "Original Packet" section to mean the connection from the client to the server: before any policy actions.

Let's say an Internet user in Fresno, CA, is browsing to your website (web.lab.com) at IP address 1.1.2.1 in Washington DC. Also, for clarification, 1.1.2.1 is the public IP address on your firewall, which will accept the incoming connection, translate the destination IP address to the internal true IP address of the server, and then send the flow on its way. The user in Fresno, sitting behind his or her ISP router with NAT enabled, will source traffic from a public IP address of let's say 2.2.2.1. So, the original packet, from your boundary firewall's perspective, is:

Source: (2.2.2.1 zone: Internet)   Destination: (1.1.2.1 zone: Internet)

I used zone "Internet" in the example above just to prove the point that your NAT policy "Original Packet" configuration needs to match the original packet.

So, you'll also notice that when you configure destination NAT if using your firewall's public IP address to allow outside clients in, the source and destination zones will, more than likely, be the same, and your destination IP address will be the original destination address before translation. How could this be different? Well, if the destination address, being a publicly reachable IP address, happens to reside on an interface besides the inbound "Internet-facing" firewall interface, and, this other interface is associated with a different zone, it will cause the destination NAT "Original Packet" configuration to deviate from the norm. Why would you do this? Well, if you wanted to avoid having traffic processed at your outside Internet-facing interface, and instead you wanted to have the traffic cross the firewall security stack before translation, using this option would accomplish that goal. However, having a spare public IP address available to ensure reachability from the outside is another problem altogether. This option is meant to show you how much flexibility you have with NAT configurations. For clarification, here are a couple of figures to give you a better idea.

Typical Destination NAT "Original Packet" Configuration

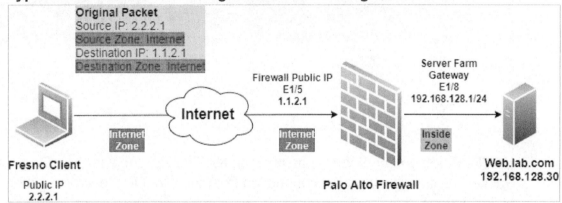

Atypical Destination NAT "Original Packet" Configuration

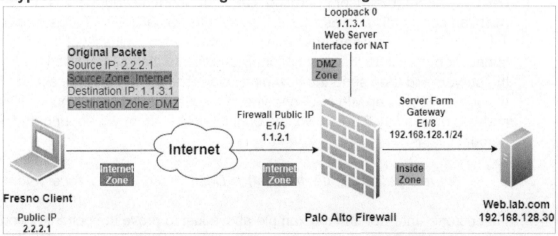

Now, when you make a security policy to allow translated traffic, unlike when you created the NAT policy, you'll need to change the destination zone to the actual zone that the traffic will take…the exit zone. You'll still list the destination IP as the original public IP address. The short answer for why this is the case: the required security policy setting for translated destination traffic is the result of the order in which the firewall processes the packet. The step for selecting a security policy match happens before the actual translation of the destination address;

however, routing is determined, and the true zones are identified before the security policy match. Here's a general outline of the process.

1. Initial Packet Processing: Routing and NAT Policy evaluated
2. Security Pre-Policy, Application, and Security Policy processes completed
3. Post Policy Processing: NAT Policy Applied

Also, here's the "High-Level" diagram from Palo Alto Networks outlining all the firewall packet processing steps.

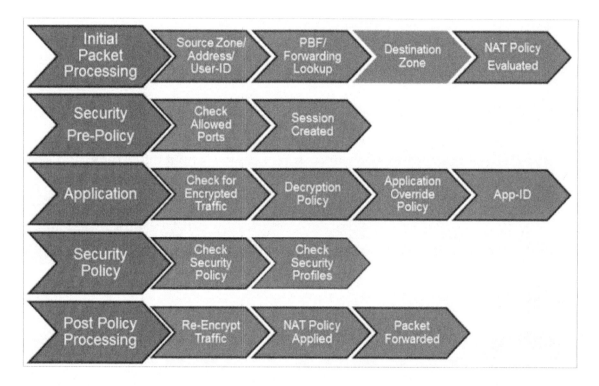

For a quick example, my traffic (which I will be using in the future configuration examples), coming from 1.1.2.2 is destined for 1.1.2.1. Both of these IPs are considered to be within the Guest zone (the same would hold true for the outside interface and an Internet client connecting inbound…based on the default route, the firewall considers your outside interface and all clients on the Internet to be in the same zone. Of course, this makes sense, but if you've never considered it before, it might seem strange initially.

Alright, that's plenty of information on destination NAT policy processing. Let's configure this.
Select the "Original Packet" tab, add the "Source Zone" (in my case, "Guest"), select the "Destination Zone" (in my case, "Guest"), add a port to the "Service"

dropdown box (in my case, TCP-443), and finally add the "Destination Address" (in my case, 1.1.2.1).

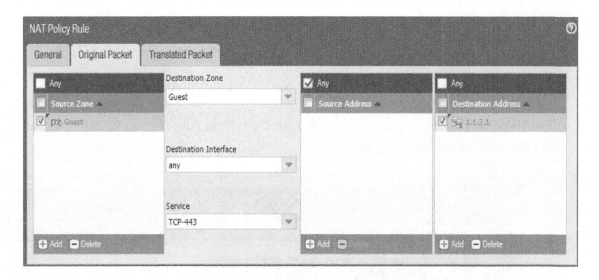

Lastly, click on the "Translated Packet" tab, select "Translation Type" as "Static IP" under the "Destination Address Translation", input the "Translated Address" (in my case, 192.168.128.30), and then click "OK" and Commit the config.

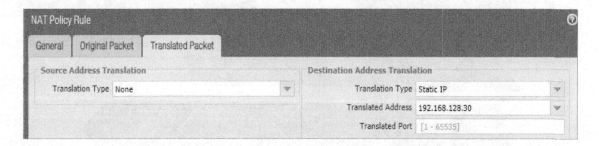

Now, for the "Guest" client to use the public IP (1.1.2.1) and not resolve to the 192.168.128.30 address or any other address for that matter, go ahead and add an entry into your "hosts" file, and then do a quick ping to make sure it's resolving to the new IP.

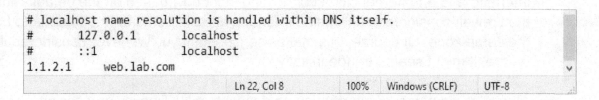

```
    Command Prompt
Microsoft Windows [Version 10.0.18363.778]
(c) 2019 Microsoft Corporation. All rights reserved.

C:\Users\domain.admin>ping web.lab.com

Pinging web.lab.com [1.1.2.1] with 32 bytes of data:
Reply from 1.1.2.1: bytes=32 time=1ms TTL=64
```

Now, once you're ready, try and browse to the internal resource (in my case, I'm using my internal webserver "web.lab.com"). You should successfully connect.

Lastly, in the firewall, go to the Monitor tab, select the Traffic link from the left-hand column, and input the following filter in the search form field: adjusted for your specific source and destination IPs.

- (addr.src in 1.1.2.2) and (addr.dst in 1.1.2.1)

Once you find the flow to TCP-443, click on the Details icon to open the "Detailed Log View" page. You'll notice that your destination zone, unlike the destination zone you configured in the NAT policy "Original Packet", is different (in my case, "Farm"). This is the point I was making earlier. When it comes to the security policy, you need the actual source and destination zones of the traffic, but the destination IP, for the security policy, must be set to the "Original Packet" IP address (in my case, 1.1.2.1).

Detailed Log View

General		Source		Destination	
Session ID	54460	Source User		Destination User	
Action	allow	Source	1.1.2.2	Destination	1.1.2.1
Action Source	from-policy	Country	China	Country	China
Application	ssl	Port	49954	Port	443
Rule	Guest-Out	Zone	Guest	Zone	Farm
Rule UUID	aaa31e19-8372-4fd6-912b-0e458f3b3fc6	Interface	ethernet1/5.2000	Interface	ethernet1/8
		NAT IP	1.1.2.2	NAT IP	192.168.128.30
Session End Reason	tcp-fin	NAT Port	49954	NAT Port	443
Category	LAB				

Alright, we have one last tool in the NAT realm to explore. Consider this: you have just completed a rollout of your new company website, using company-owned infrastructure, and you purchased a great domain name and configured public DNS records so that it could be resolved by any host on the Internet to reach the company's public IP address for this website. Everything seems perfect, then you start getting reports from within your company that the new website isn't reachable via the company network. What's the deal? Well, if your clients are receiving a DNS query answer with the company's public-facing IP address as the host, they won't be able to connect, but no worries…we've got a solution for it.

Section 3.3: U-Turn NAT (Hairpin NAT)

U-Turn NAT is a very interesting concept. The name describes the flow of traffic: the flow heads outbound, is intercepted by the NAT policy, and makes a U-turn towards the internal resource. Its usefulness lies in a situation where your client receives a DNS answer, for an internal resource, but the answer turns out to be the public IP address that Internet clients use to connect to the resource. In this case, you set a NAT policy with the source zone matching the internal client zone, a destination zone matching the public IP address interface zone, a destination address of the public IP address, and lastly a destination "translated" address to the actual resource's internal IP address. It's the same scenario as the "Atypical" destination NAT example. If you think about it, "Original Packet" means just that: the original packet header (source/destination IP addresses) and where it would go without any changes. Once you understand that, NAT policies become very easy to configure.

In this example, I am going to make up a public IP address for this. I will use 203.203.203.203, which will translate to 192.168.128.30. You do not have to use an actual configured IP address/subnet for this to work. You only need to make sure that the IP, based on routing, is reachable via the specific zone where translation will take place. When I attempt to connect to 203.203.203.203, my firewall will agree on my policy that this address resides in the "Outside" zone, and it will match and translate as needed. Again, Palo Alto Networks provides so much flexibility in configuring NAT policies.

NOTE: You need to put your U-Turn policies above your Source NAT policies. If you don't your browsing activity to the public IP address will get "Source translated" and proceed outbound to the Internet, versus performing the U-turn.

Select the Policies tab at the top, select the NAT link in the left-hand column, and click Add at the bottom. Give your policy a name (in my case, I'm using "Guest_WebServer_203.203.203.203").

Next, select the "Original Packet" tab at the top, then input the "Source Zone" (in my case, "Guest"), select the "Destination Zone" (in my case, "Outside"), set the "Service" to TCP-443 (didn't make a note of this earlier, but you need to create

51

an object for the NAT "Service" setting or use the "service-https" default option), then input your original destination IP address (in my case, 203.203.203.203).

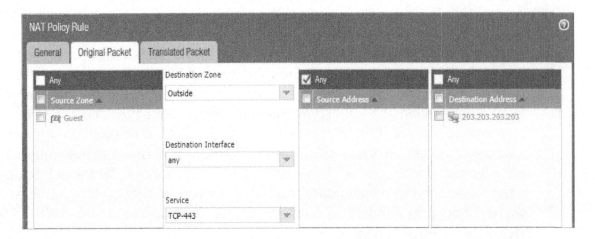

Lastly, select the "Translated Packet" tab, within the "Destination Address Translation" section, for the "Translation Type" dropdown box, select "Static IP", then input the translated IP address in the "Translated Address" form field (in my case, 192.168.128.30). Once you're finished, click "OK" to close the configuration page. Make sure the U-turn NAT policy is above the Source NAT policy, and then Commit the config.

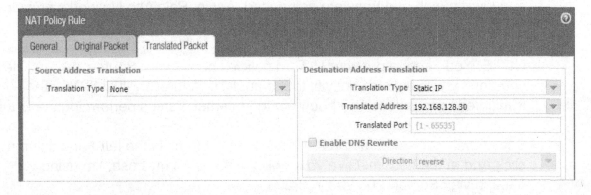

Now, to make browsing work properly, go to your client, open the "hosts" file, and update the IP address mapping for your internal web resource to 203.203.203.203. Once you save the file, attempt to browse to your internal resource (in my case, https://web.lab.com). You should connect successfully.

```
# localhost name resolution is handled within DNS itself.
#       127.0.0.1       localhost
#       ::1             localhost
203.203.203.203     web.lab.com
```
Ln 22, Col 30   100%   Windows (CRLF)   UTF-8

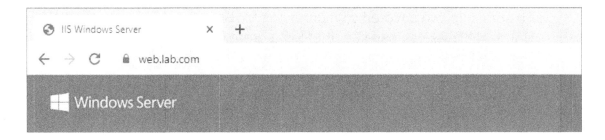

Lastly, go into the firewall, select the Monitor tab at the top, select the Traffic link in the left-hand column, and input the following filter: adjusted for your particular source and destination IPs.

- (addr.src in 1.1.2.2) and (addr.dst in 203.203.203.203)

Once the logs show up, click on the Details icon to open the "Detailed Log View" page. You'll notice that the destination address is 203.203.203.203, but instead of the destination zone showing "Outside", it is now set to "Farm", and the "NAT IP" is set to 192.168.128.30. We didn't perform any port manipulation, so it came in as TCP-443, and it passed through the NAT policy as TCP-443.

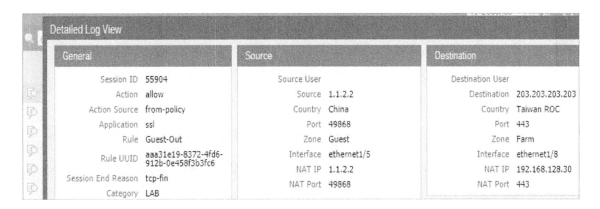

The only thing I would like to add is what you should do when your client and destination internal resource reside behind the same firewall Layer3 interface. In that case, you need to add a Source NAT configuration, within the same U-turn NAT policy, and update the source address to that of the internal firewall Layer3 address. In a sense, you're making sure the firewall continues to proxy the connection. If the server were to receive the client IP, and it did not prefer the firewall path to route back towards the client, this would disrupt the NAT process: the client expects to communicate over the established session with the public IP address, not the private one. So, with this U-turn NAT policy configuration, the client will always send traffic to the firewall to reach the public IP, and the server will always respond to the firewall Layer3 interface for return traffic: keeping the firewall in the path.

To sum it up, we covered configurations for Source NAT, Destination NAT, and U-turn NAT. As you can see, there is a great deal of flexibility when it comes to Palo NAT policy configurations. There are also many options I did not cover, so use this chapter as a guide to explore further. Now that NAT is configured, and we're able to access Internet resources, let's take our layer3 configuration even further with multicast.

Chapter 4: Palo Multicast

I love multicast, and you should too. It's super easy to work with. In any multicast deployment, the most important thing is to make sure your unicast deployment is set up correctly. When configured correctly, multicast will come alive and spread throughout your network. Simply put: If everyone is reachable, multicast routing and protocol independent multicast (PIM) are both enabled, and you are using dense mode to flood multicast everywhere, it will work. With that said, don't ever use dense mode. You can end up needlessly flooding multicast streams everywhere, even when no one is joined. Instead, establish a rendezvous point (RP) and switch to sparse mode. In the basic sense, sparse mode relies on a central point that aggregates all sources of streams and all receiver join requests. Once a receiver asks the RP for a specific group, the RP will provide the unicast source of the stream. At that point, the last hop router (LHR) will establish a connection direct to the source, or first-hop router (FHR) using unicast routing and pull the stream down to the receiver.

The initial request from the source to the RP is called a PIM register. The source announces it is available, and the RP responds by joining the group and installing a "source comma group" (S,G) route, then the RP creates a "star comma group" (*.G) route entry. The (S,G) is called the shortest path tree, and the (*,G) is called the shared tree. Why? Because any number of sources can register with the RP for the same group, building multiple shortest path trees. Then, when receivers request the group and the LHR generates and sends the PIM join, it does so for the (*,G) route: not knowing the source, but expecting the RP to provide that information. All receivers first join this group, the shared tree, but depending on the receiver location within the network, not all receivers will join the same (S,G) route since the choice of a (S,G) is based on shortest path (based on routing protocol metrics) between the source and receiver.

Section 4.1: General Multicast Operation (PIM Sparse Mode)

Let's walk through some examples. In the topology figure below, 192.168.128.222 is beginning a stream to group address 239.1.1.1.

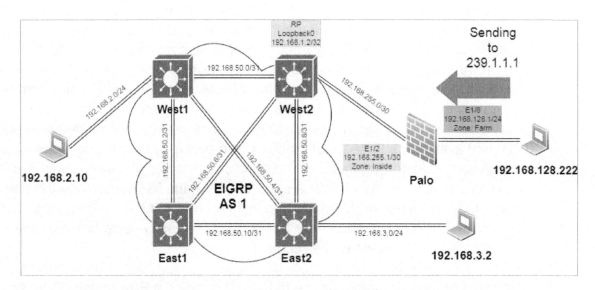

This is a packet capture of the sender traffic at the first hop (Palo interface Ethernet 1/8). As you can see, it is a raw UDP MPEG stream to group address 239.1.1.1.

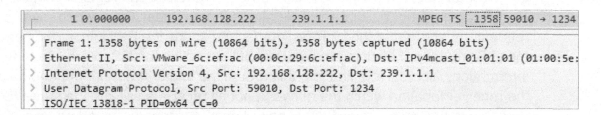

Next, the Palo generates a PIM register and forwards this via unicast from incoming interface (Eth1/8 – 192.168.128.1) to the RP (192.168.1.2).

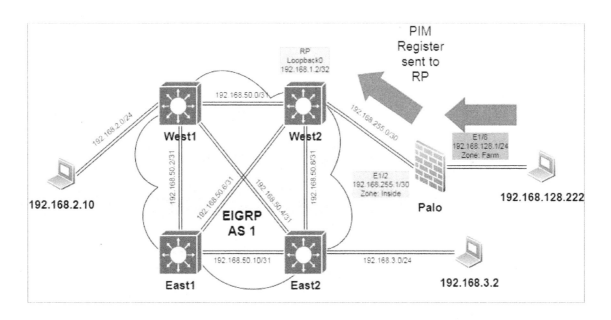

As you can see in the packet capture below, the Palo sent a PIM register to the RP. Interesting to note: Wireshark shows the source as 192.168.128.222 and the destination as 239.1.1.1, but if you look at the entire frame, it appears similar to a generic routing encapsulation (GRE) packet, where the outer IP header (Source: 192.168.128.1, Destination: 192.168.1.2) lists the next protocol as PIM, followed by a PIM header and then an additional IP header inside. Then, the RP sends a register stop back to the source FHR (192.168.128.1).

```
   117 35.305490    192.168.128.222    239.1.1.1       PIMv2    1390 Register
   110 35 305490    192 168 128 222    239 1 1 1       DIM.2    1390 Dagiston
>  Frame 117: 1390 bytes on wire (11120 bits), 1390 bytes captured (11120 bits) on inter
>  Ethernet II, Src: PaloAlto_83:bc:11 (08:30:6b:83:bc:11), Dst: Cisco_e8:94:42 (00:1e:4
>  Internet Protocol Version 4, Src: 192.168.128.1, Dst: 192.168.1.2
>  Protocol Independent Multicast
>  Internet Protocol Version 4, Src: 192.168.128.222, Dst: 239.1.1.1
```

```
   208 36.154596    192.168.1.2       192.168.128.1    PIMv2
   200 36 155062    102 168 1 2       102 168 128 1    DTM.2
>  Internet Protocol Version 4, Src: 192.168.1.2, Dst: 192.168.128.1
∨  Protocol Independent Multicast
     0010 .... = Version: 2
     .... 0010 = Type: Register-stop (2)
     Reserved byte(s): 00
     Checksum: 0xaa55 [correct]
     [Checksum Status: Good]
  ∨  PIM Options
        Group: 239.1.1.1/32
        Source: 192.168.128.222
```

If you look at the multicast routing table of the RP device (West2), you will see two entries.

```
WEST2#show ip mroute | sec 239.1.1.1
(*, 239.1.1.1), 00:10:32/stopped, RP 192.168.1.2, flags: SP
  Incoming interface: Null, RPF nbr 0.0.0.0
  Outgoing interface list: Null
(192.168.128.222, 239.1.1.1), 00:10:32/00:02:03, flags: P
  Incoming interface: Vlan255, RPF nbr 192.168.255.1
  Outgoing interface list: Null
```

Remember, as I said previously, the (S,G) and (*,G) route combinations facilitate multiple sources for the same group. There are two major components to see in the "show ip mroute" output: "RPF nbr" and "Outgoing interface list" (OIL for short). Since the RP creates the (*,G) route, the RPF is 0.0.0.0 (this device), but if you look at the (S,G) route, the RPF is 192.168.255.1 (the Palo Zone: Inside interface). As for the OIL, no receivers have requested to join, so the list is "Null", and the stream is pruned.

Now, from 192.168.2.10, I will join the group address 239.1.1.1.

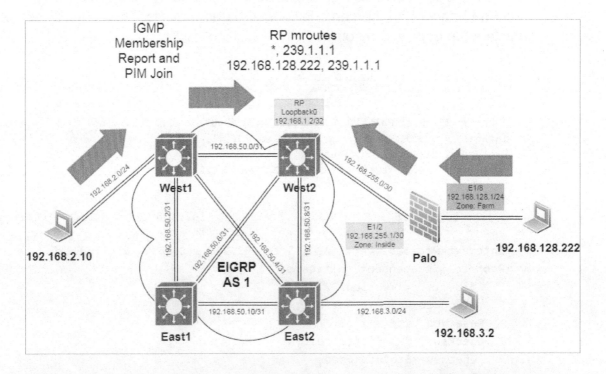

In the packet capture, you can see the IGMPv2 Membership Report where the client 192.168.2.10 is requesting group 239.1.1.1.

```
79 6.533712      192.168.2.10      239.1.1.1      IGMPv2    46 Membership Report
80 6.584556      192.168.2.1       224.0.0.102    HSRPv2    94 Hello (state Activ
81 6.630325      192.168.128.222   239.1.1.1      MPEG TS 1358 59010 → 1234 Len=1
```

```
> Frame 79: 46 bytes on wire (368 bits), 46 bytes captured (368 bits) on interface \Device\NPF_{
> Ethernet II, Src: VMware_1f:6e:90 (00:0c:29:1f:6e:90), Dst: IPv4mcast_01:01:01 (01:00:5e:01:01
> Internet Protocol Version 4, Src: 192.168.2.10, Dst: 239.1.1.1
∨ Internet Group Management Protocol
     [IGMP Version: 2]
     Type: Membership Report (0x16)
     Max Resp Time: 0.0 sec (0x00)
     Checksum: 0xf9fc [correct]
     [Checksum Status: Good]
     Multicast Address: 239.1.1.1
```

On the RP, you can see the join come in. The RP joins the inbound interface (VLAN 500 – 192.168.50.0) to both the (*,G) and (S,G) groups.

```
Aug  5 15:49:25.260: PIM(0): Received v2 Join/Prune on Vlan500 from 192.168.50.0
, to us
Aug  5 15:49:25.260: PIM(0): Join-list: (*, 239.1.1.1), RPT-bit set, WC-bit set,
 S-bit set
Aug  5 15:49:25.260: PIM(0): Add Vlan500/192.168.50.0 to (*, 239.1.1.1), Forward
 state, by PIM *G Join
Aug  5 15:49:25.260: PIM(0): Add Vlan500/192.168.50.0 to (192.168.128.222, 239.1
.1.1), Forward state, by PIM *G Join
```

Now, if you look at the RP multicast routing table, you'll see that the OIL is populated with VLAN 500.

```
WEST2#show ip mroute | sec 239.1.1.1
(*, 239.1.1.1), 00:45:11/00:03:24, RP 192.168.1.2, flags: S
  Incoming interface: Null, RPF nbr 0.0.0.0
  Outgoing interface list:
    Vlan500, Forward/Sparse, 00:00:10/00:03:24
(192.168.128.222, 239.1.1.1), 00:45:11/00:03:28, flags: T
  Incoming interface: Vlan255, RPF nbr 192.168.255.1
  Outgoing interface list:
    Vlan500, Forward/Sparse, 00:00:10/00:03:24
```

Also, if you look at the multicast routing table in the LHR (West1), you will see two entries with an RPF nbr set towards the RP (*,G) and source (S,G). Notice also that the (*,G) route lists the RP since this route is created by the RP.

```
WEST1#show ip mroute | sec 239.1.1.1
(*, 239.1.1.1), 00:29:52/00:00:47, RP 192.168.1.2, flags: SJC
  Incoming interface: Vlan500, RPF nbr 192.168.50.1
  Outgoing interface list:
    Vlan200, Forward/Sparse, 00:02:20/00:02:58
(192.168.128.222, 239.1.1.1), 00:02:18/00:02:57, flags: JT
  Incoming interface: Vlan500, RPF nbr 192.168.50.1
  Outgoing interface list:
    Vlan200, Forward/Sparse, 00:02:18/00:02:58
```

Ok, that was a lot of demonstration, and you could do a lot more analysis and testing, but I think this is enough to give you a fairly good idea of what is going on with the traffic as it pertains to multicast. So, with that said, let's look at the configuration and see how the Palo handles this traffic.

Section 4.2: Multicast Configuration

First, I need to explain that my network core consists of four Cisco 3560-8pc desktop switches interconnected in a full mesh and using EIGRP for the routing protocol. I have multicast routing enabled and PIM spare-mode configured on all layer3 interfaces. Also, the RP (192.168.1.2) is configured with the Bootstrap Router (BSR) protocol for dynamic RP advertisements. Here is a capture of the relevant information in the RP.

```
WEST2#sh run | inc multicast-routing
ip multicast-routing distributed
WEST2#show ip pim interface

Address          Interface            Ver/   Nbr    Query  DR     DR
                                      Mode   Count  Intvl  Prior
192.168.100.1    Vlan100              v2/S   0      30     1      192.168.100.1
192.168.255.2    Vlan255              v2/S   1      30     1      192.168.255.2
192.168.50.1     Vlan500              v2/S   1      30     1      192.168.50.1
192.168.50.6     Vlan503              v2/S   1      30     1      192.168.50.7
192.168.50.8     Vlan504              v2/S   1      30     1      192.168.50.9
192.168.1.2      Loopback0            v2/S   0      30     1      192.168.1.2
WEST2#sh run | inc candidate
ip pim bsr-candidate Loopback0 0
ip pim rp-candidate Loopback0
```

If I query, say EAST1 to see what RP is cached, I will see 192.168.1.2.

```
EAST1#show ip pim bsr-router
PIMv2 Bootstrap information
  BSR address: 192.168.1.2 (?)
  Uptime:       2d00h, BSR Priority: 0, Hash mask length: 0
  Expires:      00:01:57
EAST1#show ip pim rp mapping
PIM Group-to-RP Mappings

Group(s) 224.0.0.0/4
  RP 192.168.1.2 (?), v2
    Info source: 192.168.1.2 (?), via bootstrap, priority 0, holdtime 150
         Uptime: 1d23h, expires: 00:02:13
```

This is great. I have an RP dynamically learned throughout my network. PIM sparse mode will work, except, I have a Palo firewall in between my Inside and Farm zones, and I want to stream from the server farm (Farm zone) into my network. How can I do this? Let's find out.

Here's a rough outline of the topology we're working with. You can see the multilayer switches, interconnected, with West2 providing to link to the Palo within zone "Inside". Then, on the other side of the Palo, you can see the link to the streaming server within the "Farm" zone.

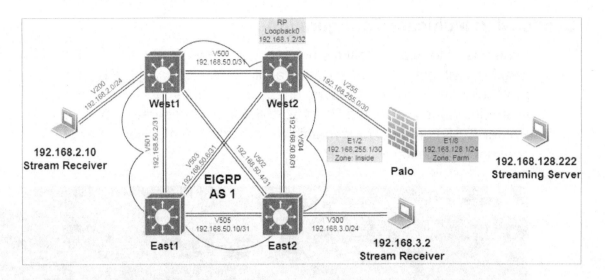

So, since my RP is learned dynamically through the network, I want the Palo to learn it dynamically as well.

The multicast configuration begins on the virtual router. If you're not using layer3 interfaces, you can forego this portion of the config. Select the Network tab at the top, then select the Virtual Routers link in the left-hand column. Once the page loads, click on and open the virtual router that your interfaces are assigned to (in my case, virtual router "VR"). Once the configuration box opens, select the "Multicast" tab on the left. For the "Rendezvous Point" tab, check the box at the top to Enable multicast and leave the local RP type set to none.

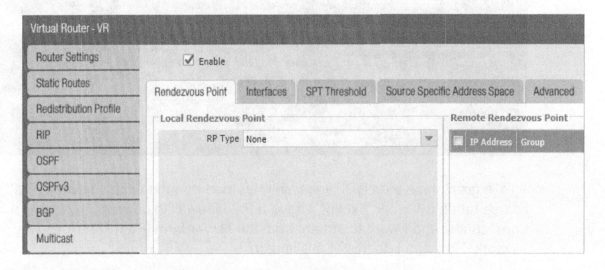

Next, click on the "Interfaces" tab, then click Add. Once the "Virtual Router – Multicast – Interface Group" page opens, click Add in the Interface box and add the interfaces that you want to participate in multicast. In my case, I'm selecting ethernet1/2 (Zone: Inside) and ethernet1/8 (Zone: Farm).

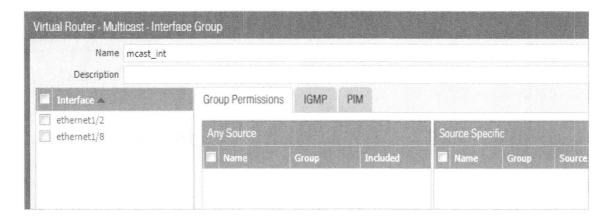

Then, select the IGMP tab. Now, as it pertains to IGMP, you only need this enabled on an interface that will have clients attempting to join a group. In my case, my Farm zone does have directly connected clients, so I will enable it. The fact that it will be enabled on my Inside zone interface is a non-issue for me, but you can break this up by creating multiple interface groups. Go ahead and select IGMP Version 2. IGMP version 3 is specifically designed for source-specific multicast (SSM), in which the client not only sends the group address to join, but it also sends the unicast address of the source. SSM is not widely used, and up to this point in my career, I've never seen it used. You can leave the other settings at their default values.

Lastly, select the PIM tab and make sure the Enable box is checked. Then click OK to close out the interface group configuration box, click OK to close out the virtual router configuration box, and then commit the config.

Now that we've enabled multicast in the Palo, let's check to see if we have a PIM neighbor. In the CLI, you can type "show routing multicast PIM neighbor" to view this information.

```
jbworley79@PA-220> show routing multicast pim neighbor

VIRTUAL ROUTER:  VR

interface         address          secondary address up time       expiry time
---------         -------          ----------------- -------       -----------
ethernet1/2       192.168.255.2    0.0.0.0                179153.63 83.13
```

As you can see in the figure above, I have a PIM neighbor (192.168.255.1), which is the switch "West2" connected to the Palo Inside zone interface. Perfect. So, what about the dynamic RP? You can check for a dynamically learned RP by typing in "show routing multicast pim elected-bsr". Also, you can type in "show routing multicast pim group-mapping" to see what group addresses the RP is configured to handle.

```
jbworley79@PA-220> show routing multicast pim elected-bsr

VIRTUAL ROUTER:   VR

elected-bsr address:         192.168.1.2
priority:                    0
hash mask length:            0
expiry time:                 105.98 seconds

jbworley79@PA-220> show routing multicast pim group-mapping

VIRTUAL ROUTER:  VR

group             RP               origin   pim mode inactive
-----             --               ------   -------- --------
232.0.0.0/8       0.0.0.0          CONFIG   SSM      no
224.0.0.0/4       192.168.1.2      BSR      ASM      no
```

The figure above is very telling. 192.168.1.2 was elected as the BSR, and as you can see, this RP is configured to handle group addresses 224.0.0.0 through 239.255.255.255 (all Class D multicast group addresses). Also notice that there is an entry for 232.0.0.0/8. This is the reserved address range for SSM, which doesn't need an RP since the receiver explicitly identifies the source unicast address. Lastly, origin shows SSM is part of the CONFIG, and any source multicast (ASM – same as PIM sparse mode) originated from the BSR. This is perfect. Let's start streaming and see what happens. I will stream from 192.168.128.222 to group address 239.1.1.1. After the stream starts, if I go back to the Palo CLI and type in "show routing multicast pim state", I see the group address and the source listed.

```
jbworley79@PA-220> show routing multicast pim state

VIRTUAL ROUTER:  VR

(S, G):

group              source            up time      upstream nbr      upstream join st
g st               DR reg stop timer    SPT
-----              ------            -------      -----------       ----------------
----               ----------------  ---
239.1.1.1          192.168.128.222   112851.51    0.0.0.0           Joined
                   0.00              yes
```

Next, I will go to the RP and check to see if I have a multicast route entry for 239.1.1.1.

```
WEST2#show ip mroute | sec 239.1.1.1
(*, 239.1.1.1), 1d07h/00:03:05, RP 192.168.1.2, flags: S
  Incoming interface: Null, RPF nbr 0.0.0.0
  Outgoing interface list:
    Vlan500, Forward/Sparse, 1d07h/00:03:05
WEST2#
```

Ah, I have a (*,G) route, but it looks like the register process did not complete, for if it did, I would also have an (S,G) listing 192.168.128.222 as the source. Alright, let's check the traffic log in the firewall for this traffic. In this case, I will input the filter (addr.dst in 239.1.1.1) and see what I find.

(addr.dst in 239.1.1.1)

Source User	To Port	From Zone	To Zone	Source	Destination	Action	Rule
	1234	Farm		192.168.128.222	239.1.1.1	drop	Deny_Any

And, we're getting dropped. Notice something interesting in this log? The "To Zone" is empty. This is indicative of Multicast traffic. When you create a security policy, you have options for the destination zone, one of which is "multicast". Let's configure a security policy to get this running. Select the Policies tab at the top of the Palo web GUI, select the Security link in the left-hand column, then click Add at the bottom of the page.

NOTE: Make sure to place this rule above any "Deny" rules that might match the traffic.

For the sake of brevity, I won't cover the full security policy configuration. However, here is an example of the destination zone drop-down box where you can choose "multicast", "any", or "select" to choose a specific zone. I will choose "multicast" of course.

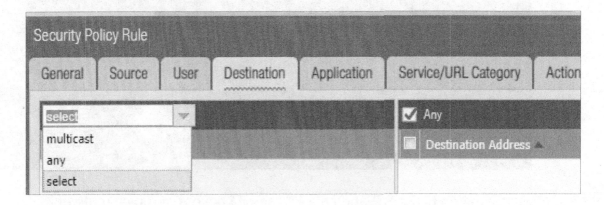

Here's an example of the config.

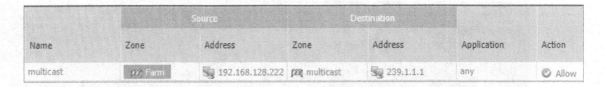

As you can see, traffic from "Farm – 192.168.128.222" to "multicast – 239.1.1.1" is allowed. Now, I will commit this config, check the Palo traffic log, and check the RP again to see if I get my (S,G) route.

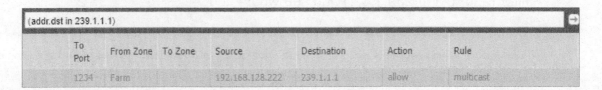

```
WEST2#show ip mroute | sec 239.1.1.1
(*, 239.1.1.1), 1d07h/00:02:48, RP 192.168.1.2, flags: S
  Incoming interface: Null, RPF nbr 0.0.0.0
  Outgoing interface list:
    Vlan500, Forward/Sparse, 1d07h/00:02:48
(192.168.128.222, 239.1.1.1), 00:01:32/00:03:21, flags: T
  Incoming interface: Vlan255, RPF nbr 192.168.255.1
  Outgoing interface list:
    Vlan500, Forward/Sparse, 00:01:32/00:02:56
```

The traffic log shows that the traffic was allowed, and the RP now has an (S,G) route. Alright, now I will try and join this group from 192.168.2.10.

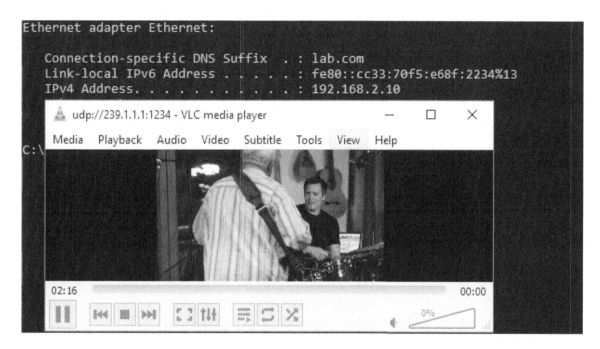

My client successfully pulled the stream, proving that my multicast-enabled network, with the Palo included, worked as intended.

This configuration example should give you a pretty go idea of how to configure the Palo to handle, and participate in, multicast streams. There are many features you can enable on the virtual router, and you can even set the Palo to be the RP, although that would not be a typical configuration, it does provide the option. One word of caution: the Palo will not participate in AutoRP (cisco proprietary dynamic RP configuration). This isn't a showstopper, since the Palo works with BSR, and if nothing else, you can configure the Palo with a static remote RP if needed.

I hope you find this chapter helpful. Multicast seems to be an esoteric topic among most IT professionals, but if you follow a few simple rules during setup, it's very easy to maintain and troubleshoot. Now that our layer3 configuration is maxed out, let's prepare our firewall to decrypt traffic for inspection.

Chapter 5: Forward Proxy Decryption

Decryption is an integral component of any firewall intrusion detection and prevention system. Mostly all Internet-based flows are contained within a transport layer security (TLS) tunnel. Also, understand that this technology is also commonly referred to as Secure Sockets Layer (SSL). According to https://sites.google.com/site/tlsssloverview/history, "SSL was originally developed by Netscape in 1994…Later the IETF (Internet Engineering Task Force) developed a standardize[d] protocol to provide the same functionality: TLS". So, just know that SSL and TLS are terms used interchangeably to describe the same concept. Alright, so TLS causes a major issue for network security systems. If the flow is secured in an encrypted tunnel that only the client and server are capable of deciphering, anything can pass along the path with zero visibility from the outside: no detection of viruses, spyware, known exploits, or zero-day vulnerabilities, etc. So, to solve this issue, we must implement decryption.

Forward Proxy Decryption enables us to see inside the tunnel, safely and securely via the control plane of the firewall, so that we can act upon any malicious traffic using AppID and URL category matching, as well as content inspection. Also, security engineers can set up "Decrypt Mirror" ports, which function similarly as switch port analyzer (SPAN) ports, but only forwarding the decrypted traffic out of a firewall port to analyze the traffic out-of-band (OOB) using third-party tools. I cannot provide an example of decrypt mirroring. The PA-220 does not offer this feature, but I still wanted to make you aware of the option if you're using a 3000/3200 series or greater version of Palo hardware.

In this chapter, we will enable the certificate, we created back in Chapter 1, for Forward Proxy Trust, then we'll configure a decryption policy to decrypt our Internet-bound traffic. Lastly, I'll touch on the decryption profile and how it can further enhance security for TLS traffic traversing your firewall.

Alright, let's begin.

Section 5.1: Configure the Forward Proxy Certificates

First, click on the Device tab. Then, under the Certificate Management section, click the dropdown arrow and select the Certificates link. Then, click on the certificate you created in Chapter 1 (in my case, "firewall") to open the "Certificate information" configuration page.

You'll notice two checkboxes near the bottom.

- Forward Trust Certificate
- Forward Untrust Certificate

The "Forward Trust Certificate" is the certificate the firewall uses to sign the server certificate when the firewall trusts the server's original certificate. This means the firewall validated:

- The server name indication matched one of the alternative names in the cert
- The server cert was within the validity period: valid from, valid to
- The server cert was signed by a root CA that the firewall trusts
- If configured to check certificate revocation, the firewall confirmed with the root CA server that the certificate had not been revoked

So, you'll want to check the "Forward Trust Certificate" box for the certificate you created in Chapter 1, but what about the "Forward Untrust Certificate" box?

You can consider that "Forward Untrust Certificate" is used for any server certificate that doesn't match all of the criteria I listed above for the "Forward Trust Certificate" option. You can use the same certificate and enable both options, but your internal clients will see all websites trusted, regardless of whether they're using valid certificates or not. Generally, you would create a self-signed "certificate authority" certificate on the firewall and check the box for "Forward Untrust Certificate". Why? This self-signed certificate is not going to be automatically trusted throughout your internal domain, so if a website uses an invalid certificate, the firewall will issue a certificate using this self-signed CA cert, and your client will respond appropriately by identifying that the certificate is not trusted.

So, go ahead and check the box for "Forward Trust Certificate" and click "OK".

Next, on the "Device Certificates" main page, click the Generate link at the bottom. Once the "Generate Certificate" configuration page pops up, fill in the "Certificate Name" and "Common Name" fields with your name of choice, check the box for "Certificate Authority", then click "Generate" at the bottom.

You should get a dialog box saying the firewall successfully generated the certificate and key pair. Click "OK".

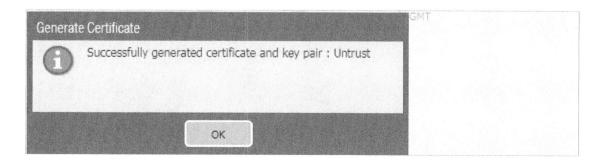

Once the dialog box closes, click on the certificate you just generated to open the "Certificate information" configuration page, and then check the box for "Forward Untrust Certificate", then click "OK" to close the box.

☑ Forward Untrust Certificate

Now, when your users browse to a web site that has an invalid certificate, the firewall will still decrypt, but it will also notify the client that the site is not trusted.

Next, we need to configure a policy to match traffic and begin decrypting flows.

Section 5.2: Configure a Decryption Policy

Select the Policies tab, and in the left-hand column, click on the Decryption link. Next, click Add at the bottom of the page. Once the "Decryption Policy Rule" configuration page comes up, give your policy a name (in my case, I'm using "Guest-Decrypt").

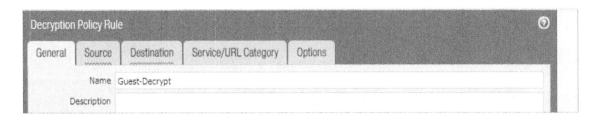

Next, select the "Source" tab, add a "Source Zone" (in my case, "Guest"), and leave the "Source Address" and "Source User" fields set to "Any".

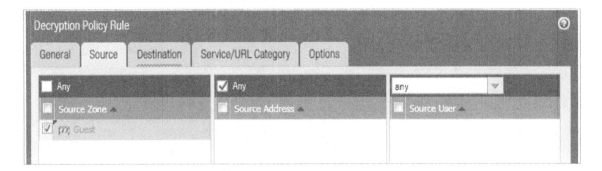

Then, select the "Destination" tab, add in your "Destination Zone" of choice (in my case, I'm using "Outside", which is my Internet-facing zone), and leave the "Destination Address" field set to "Any".

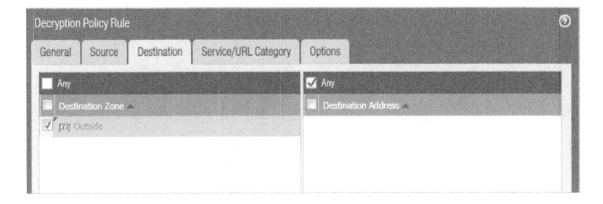

Lastly, select the "Options" tab, for the "Action" setting, select the "Decrypt" radio button, and then make sure the "Type" field is set to "SSL Forward Proxy". Once you've configured and confirmed these settings, click "OK", then Commit the config.

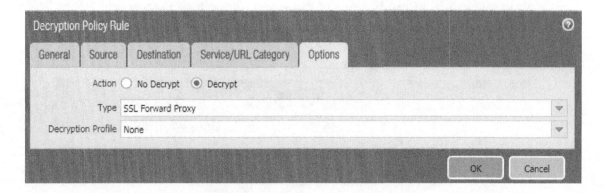

Now, with the forward proxy decryption policy in place, go to your "Guest" machine and browse to some internet website. For my example, I'll be using https://httpvshttps.com for testing decryption. Also, I have a special scenario set up to require manual intervention to get the client to trust the root certificate. Notice that when I browse to the website, I get a certificate error.

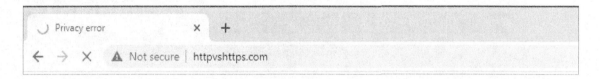

I do not have the root certificate in my trusted root certificate store. If I click on the "Not secure" notification in the address bar, then click on the "Certificate (Invalid)" link and select the "Certification Path" tab at the top, I can see that the root certificate is not trusted (the red circle with an "X" on the certificate icon tells me this root certificate was provided in the chain but is not trusted).

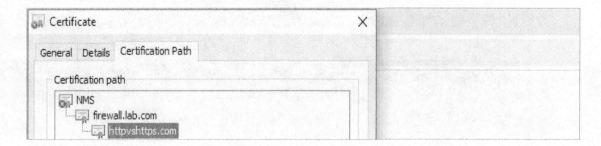

Also, if using "Chrome", open "Developer Tools", select "Security", and you'll see that the root certificate is missing.

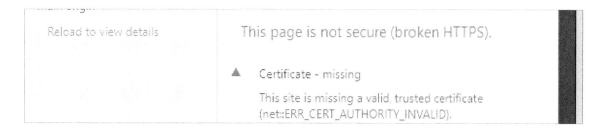

To fix this, simply select the root certificate in the "Certification Path" window and click on "View Certificate".

When the new "Certificate" window opens, click on the "Details" tab at the top, and then click on "Copy to File…" at the bottom of the window.

At this point, you will be guided through the "Certificate Export Wizard". Just make sure to select "Base-64 encoded X.509 (.CER)" for the file format. I have found that base-64 is the best option for file type since it is the most universally accepted certificate encoding option. You must use this option for importing certificates into the Palo firewall. Don't confuse this with the "certificate and private key" pair, which uses PKCS #12. I'm referring to the process of importing trusted root certificates into the firewall, which do not include a private key. Lastly, make sure you save the certificate to a location you can easily find, and make sure you give it a name that you can search for and find easily if needed. In my case, I name my certificate "NMS" after the root certificate authority hostname, and I save the file to my "Guest" client desktop.

Now, with the certificate downloaded to your client machine, double click it, select "Open" for the security dialog box, and then select "Install Certificate". Once the "Certificate Import Wizard" opens, select "Local Machine", click "Next", select "Place all certificates in the following store", click "Browse...", and select "Trusted Root Certification Authorities" and click "OK".

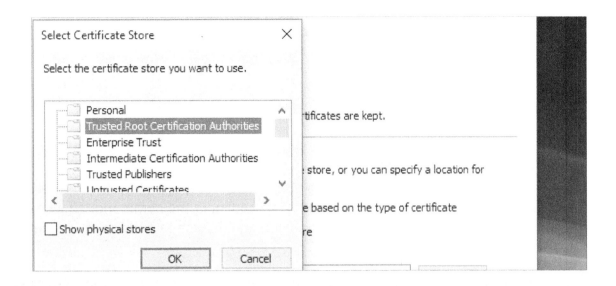

Then, click "Next", and lastly click "Finish" and then click "OK" to close out the dialog box. So, you've just trusted this root certificate, which is the root certificate that signed the website certificate. This process can be used to resolve all missing root certificate issues: root or intermediate root. In my example, the Palo subordinate CA cert was signed by the root CA "NMS". When the Palo proxied the connection, it signed the httpvshttps.com web server certificate, and it also chained the root and intermediate root (Palo subCA cert) in the server certificate response. If the Palo did not provide the entire certificate chain, I would have also needed to perform the same process for the Palo subCA certificate (firewall.lab.com) to establish trust. Just be aware that it is a best practice to trust all root and intermediate root certificates explicitly. For an example of a chained TLS server certificate response, please refer to the figure below.

```
Certificate: 308203523082023aa00302010202124ab42bc6d66550146c… (id-at-commonName=httpvshttps.com)
Certificate Length: 1283
Certificate: 308204ff308203e7a00302010202132e00000023a7dc3f0f… (id-at-commonName=firewall.lab.com)
Certificate Length: 847
Certificate: 3082034b30820233a00302010202021037b68c3bf03db49845… (id-at-commonName=NMS,dc=lab,dc=com
```

Now, if I open my "Guest" client browser and attempt to connect to https://httpvshttps.com again, I will get a trusted connection. Also, if I check the certification path, I will now see the "NMS" cert without the red circle with an "X", indicating that this root certificate is trusted.

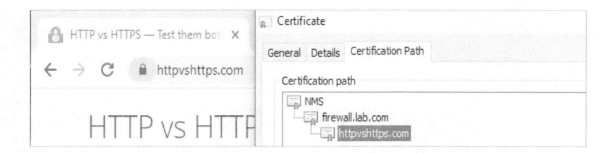

I'd like to wrap up this section with one last observation in the Palo firewall. If you log into the command-line interface (CLI) and input the command "show system setting ssl-decrypt certificate-cache", you can browse to and find the signed certificate for "httpsvshttps.com".

```
global trusted, hits: 58, refs: 1,
Root CA: 0130_DST_Root_CA_X3.cer
original cert len 2575
subject httpvshttps.com
CRL OCSP status: valid, timeout(secs): 0
original serial number(18)
04 fc 3c ee a8 3d fa 50  6c 5c 1a a1 89 bc 46 00   ..<..=.P l\....F.
59 c3                                              Y.
built x509 certificate
version 2
cert algorithm 4
valid 200507054405Z -- 200805054405Z
cert pki 1
subject: httpvshttps.com
issuer: firewall.lab.com
serial number(18)
4a b4 2b c6 d6 65 50 14  6c 5c 1a a1 89 bc 46 00   J.+..eP. l\....F.
59 c3                                              Y.
rsa key size 2048 bits siglen 256 bytes
basic constraints extension CA 0
```

In the figure above, you can see that the original root certificate for this site is "0130_DST_Root_CA_X3.cer", and it also shows the original serial number and verification via online certificate status protocol (OCSP) that this certificate is valid. Further down the figure, you'll also see "built x509 certificate". At this point, the firewall is using the contents of the original certificate to create and sign a new certificate. Also note that the "issuer" of the new certificate is "firewall.lab.com", which is the subCA certificate we previously imported and configured in the Palo firewall.

If I disable the original root certificate in the Palo root trust store (Default Trusted Certificate Authorities) and browse to httpvshttps.com again, I will get a different result.

As you can see, the forward proxy decryption process is using the "Untrust" certificate, which we previously configured to handle the decryption of flows to servers that were not trusted by the Palo firewall (Forward Untrust Certificate).

If we analyze the certificate cache, we will see this in greater detail.

```
global untrusted, hits: 0, refs: 1,
original cert len 2575
subject httpvshttps.com
CRL OCSP status: untrusted valid, timeout(secs): 0
original serial number(18)
04 fc 3c ee a8 3d fa 50  6c 5c 1a a1 89 bc 46 00   ..<..=.P 1\....F.
59 c3                                              Y.
built x509 certificate
version 2
cert algorithm 4
valid 2005070544405Z -- 2008050544405Z
cert pki 1
subject: httpvshttps.com
issuer: Untrust
serial number(18)
4a b4 2b c6 d6 65 50 14  6c 5c 1a a1 89 bc 46 00   J.+..eP. 1\....F.
59 c3                                              Y.
rsa key size 2048 bits siglen 256 bytes
basic constraints extension CA 0
```

As you can see in the figure above, there is no "Root CA" identified in the original certificate, and the "built" certificate is issued by "Untrust" since the firewall cannot verify the root certificate authority for httpvshttps.com.

Section 5.3: Configure a Decryption Profile

In this last section, we'll look at decryption profiles. As it pertains to the flow of TLS traffic, there are a couple of components involved in validating trust relationships between systems: the certificate and private key validation, and mutually accepted protocol and algorithms. We have seen the process of certificate trust in play, but for the choice of protocols, this is where Decryption Profiles make their mark. The specific protocol is a choice of SSL 3.0 through TLS 1.2. As for the algorithms, these are identified by the various stages of negotiating a secure connection: Key Exchange, Authentication, and Encryption. Decryption profiles let you define what protocols and algorithms (cipher suites) are acceptable for your organization's security policy. There are other settings available that provide a great deal of flexibility for your configuration desires, however, for this book, we will be focusing on the SSL Protocol Settings.

You can view the Decryption Profiles by navigating to the "Objects" tab, expanding the "Decryption" section in the left-hand column, and then selecting the "Decryption Profile" link.

Once you're in this section, click "Add" at the bottom of the screen, give your profile a name (in my case, I'm going to use "Guest_Decrypt"), select the "SSL Protocol Settings" tab, verify that the "Min Version" and "Max Version" is set to "TLSv1.0" and "Max" respectively, and lastly make sure that only the "MD5" checkbox is unchecked, then click "OK".

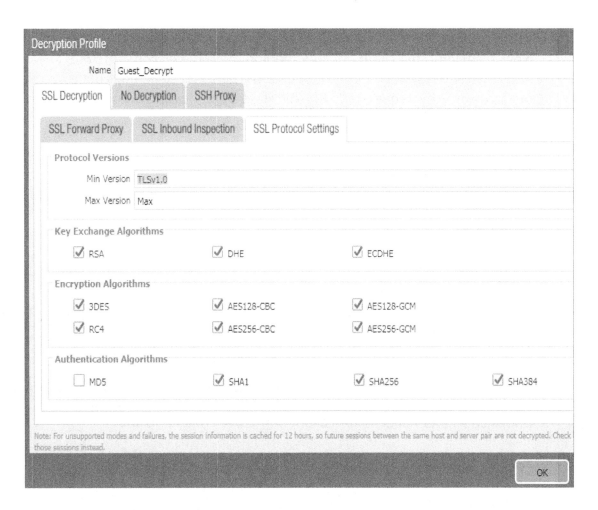

Next, navigate to the "Policies" tab, select the "Decryption" link in the left-hand column, and click on/open the policy you created earlier in this chapter (in my case, my policy is named "Guest-Decrypt"). Once the "Decryption Policy Rule" configuration window is open, select the "Options" tab, and under the "Decryption Profile" dropdown field, choose the Decryption Profile you just created, click "OK", and lastly "Commit" the config.

Now, from your test client, residing behind the "Guest" zone, browse to website https://www.yellowknife.ca using a Chrome browser. Once the page loads, enter the following key sequence "Ctrl+shift+I" to open developer tools, then open the "Security Overview" page.

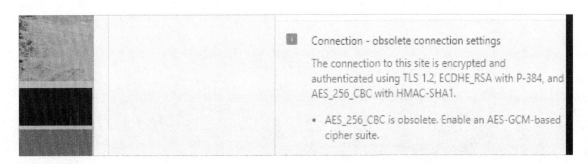

In the previous example, you can see that the web server chose to use protocol TLS1.2, key exchange algorithm ECDHE_RSA, authentication algorithm "HMAC-SHA1", and encryption algorithm "AES_256_CBC". This simply shows that out of all available cipher suites the client requested, the server chose this one. Here are a couple of packet captures to show this process in greater detail. Specifically, this will detail the client and server hello packets.

Here is the client hello listing 16 available cipher suites for the webserver to use.

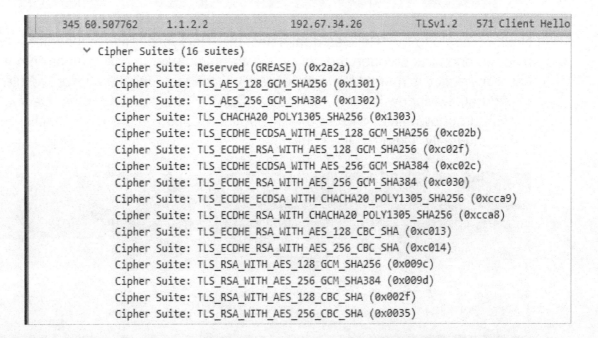

Here is the server hello from https://www.yellowknife.ca choosing the 0xc014 cipher suite (TLS_ECDHE_RSA_WITH_AES_256_CBC_SHA).

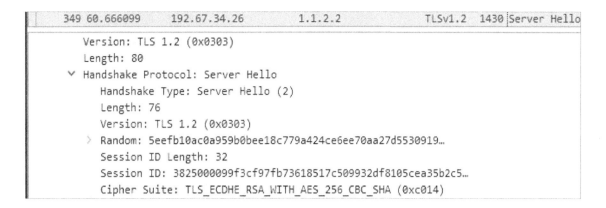

| 349 60.666099 | 192.67.34.26 | 1.1.2.2 | TLSv1.2 | 1430 | Server Hello |

```
        Version: TLS 1.2 (0x0303)
        Length: 80
      ˅ Handshake Protocol: Server Hello
            Handshake Type: Server Hello (2)
            Length: 76
            Version: TLS 1.2 (0x0303)
          › Random: 5eefb10ac0a959b0bee18c779a424ce6ee70aa27d5530919…
            Session ID Length: 32
            Session ID: 3825000099f3cf97fb73618517c509932df8105cea35b2c5…
            Cipher Suite: TLS_ECDHE_RSA_WITH_AES_256_CBC_SHA (0xc014)
```

Alright, so using the Decryption Profile, let's see if we can alter which cipher suite the server chooses to use.

Go to the Objects tab at the top, click to expand the "Decryption" section in the left-hand column, and lastly select the "Decryption Profile" link. Click on the Decryption Profile you created and applied earlier (in my case, "Guest_Decrypt"), and once the Decryption Profile configuration window comes up, select the main "SSL Decryption" tab and then select the "SSL Protocol Settings" sub-tab. Once you're there, uncheck "SHA1" under the "Authentication Algorithms" section, click "OK", and lastly Commit the config.

Now, go back to your client, browse to https://www.yellowknife.ca using Chrome, enter the key sequence "Ctrl+shift+i", select the "Security Overview" page again, and notice that the server is no longer using SHA1.

In the Decryption Profile authentication algorithms section, we still allow SHA256 and SHA384. It is apparent, however, that this website cannot support these options, so it instead depreciates the key exchange from ECDHE to RSA.

Once again, return to the Decryption Profile, and this time uncheck the box for RSA under the "Key Exchange Algorithms" section.

NOTE: When you uncheck "RSA", the web interface will automatically check the "SHA1" box again. Just uncheck it again so that RSA and SHA1 are both unchecked. "RC4" will also automatically uncheck, but there is no need for concern.

Once you are finished, click "OK" and Commit the config.

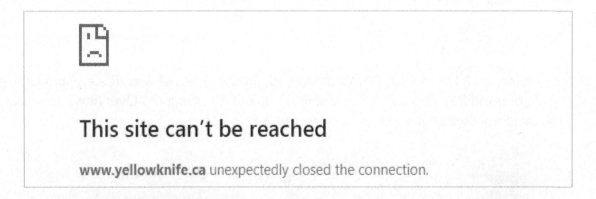

Now, return to your client and try to browse to https://www.yellowknife.ca again. This time, your connection attempt will be refused.

This site can't be reached

www.yellowknife.ca unexpectedly closed the connection.

Performing a packet capture on the client will not yield much more info. You can see in the example below, that the client sent a hello packet, listing the cipher suite options available, and the server replied with a TCP FIN to close out the connection.

```
  3491 855.140711    1.1.2.2         192.67.34.26        TLSv1    571 Client Hello
  3492 855.194637    192.67.34.26    1.1.2.2             TCP       60 443 → 62294 [FIN, ACK]
> Frame 3492: 60 bytes on wire (480 bits), 60 bytes captured (480 bits) on interface \Device\NPF_{91{
> Ethernet II, Src: PaloAlto_83:bc:14 (08:30:6b:83:bc:14), Dst: VMware_1f:6e:90 (00:0c:29:1f:6e:90)
> Internet Protocol Version 4, Src: 192.67.34.26, Dst: 1.1.2.2
> Transmission Control Protocol, Src Port: 443, Dst Port: 62294, Seq: 1, Ack: 518, Len: 0
```

We know why the server closed the connection. We modified the decryption profile to disable the use of SHA1 authentication and RSA key exchange, and as a result, the server could not establish a secure connection. But what if we had not changed anything? Remember, the firewall is decrypting the flow, so there is a secure tunnel from the client to the firewall, and there is a second tunnel from the firewall to the webserver. For us to see the full details, we need to perform a multi-stage packet capture on the firewall.

Select the Monitor tab and click on the Packet Capture link in the left-hand column. Once the page loads, click on Manage Filters and input between the web server and your client, and then input filters between the firewall global NAT address and the webserver. In my case, my client IP is 1.1.2.2, my firewall global NAT address is 10.0.0.202, and the IP for www.yellowknife.ca is 192.67.34.26. Once you have each filter created, click "OK".

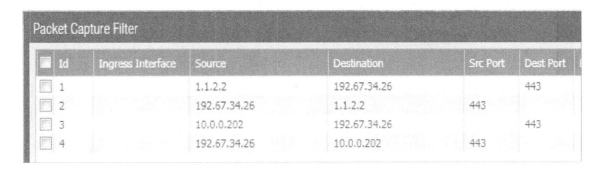

Id	Ingress Interface	Source	Destination	Src Port	Dest Port
1		1.1.2.2	192.67.34.26		443
2		192.67.34.26	1.1.2.2	443	
3		10.0.0.202	192.67.34.26		443
4		192.67.34.26	10.0.0.202	443	

Then, under the "Configure Capturing" section, click "Add" and create file names for each packet capture stage. Here's an example of the "drop" packet capture stage configuration.

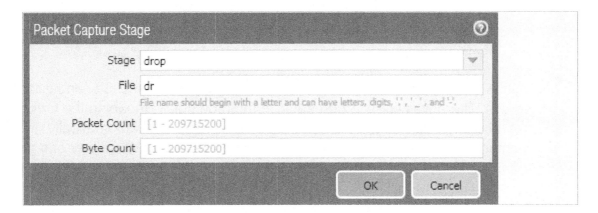

In my case, I follow a simple naming convention for each packet capture stage configuration, as you can see below.

You only need a quick way to differentiate between the different stages so you can easily distinguish between each. Once the filter and stage configuration are complete, click the switches to turn "ON" Filtering and Packet Capturing.

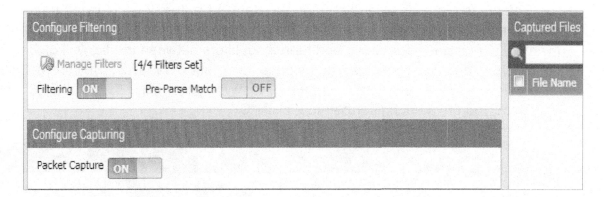

Next, go to your client and browse to https://www.yellowknife.ca. Once finished, return to the firewall packet capture page, and you should see entries in the "Capture Files" section.

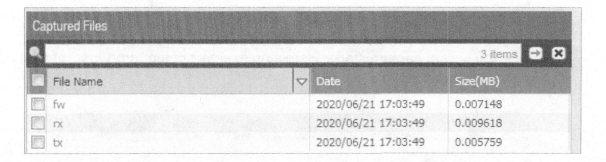

Notice that you have three files representing the firewall, receive, and transmit stages. There was no recorded traffic in the drop stage, meaning the firewall did not drop any traffic. If you click on these file names, it will automatically download them to your client. Browse to and open these files using Wireshark and review the flow.

Also, since the flow will be using your NAT policy, make sure to access the traffic log by clicking the Monitor tab and selecting the Traffic link in the left-hand column. Once the traffic log comes up, search for a flow from your client to www.yellowknife.ca.

My example: (addr.src in 1.1.2.2) and (addr.dst in 192.67.34.26)
Once you find a flow, click the Traffic Details link to the left of the log.

Detailed Log View

General		Source		Destination	
Session ID	19444	Source User		Destination User	
Action	allow	Source	1.1.2.2	Destination	192.67.34.26
Action Source	from-policy	Country	China	Country	Canada
Application	ssl	Port	62503	Port	443
Rule	Guest-Out	Zone	Guest	Zone	Outside
Rule UUID	aaa31e19-8372-4fd6-912b-0e458f3b3fc6	Interface	ethernet1/5	Interface	ethernet1/1
		NAT IP	10.0.0.202	NAT IP	192.67.34.26
Session End Reason	aged-out	NAT Port	17633	NAT Port	443
Category	any				

You'll notice that the Source section outlines the source IP and port (1.1.2.2 and 62503) as well as the NAT IP and port (10.0.0.202 and 17633). Based on this information, you can filter for pre and post NAT traffic
My example filter for Wireshark:
ip.addr == 192.67.34.26 && (tcp.port == 62503 or tcp.port == 17633)

Firewall stage packet capture

ip.addr == 192.67.34.26 && (tcp.port == 62503 or tcp.port == 17633)

No.	Time	Source	Destination	Protocol	Length	Info
1	2020-06-21 16:18:17.562965	1.1.2.2	192.67.34.26	TCP	66	62503 → 443 [SYN] Seq
3	2020-06-21 16:18:17.610907	192.67.34.26	10.0.0.202	TCP	66	443 → 17633 [SYN, ACK
4	2020-06-21 16:18:17.611382	1.1.2.2	192.67.34.26	TCP	54	62503 → 443 [ACK] Seq
5	2020-06-21 16:18:17.611932	1.1.2.2	192.67.34.26	TLSv1	571	Client Hello

Receive stage packet capture

ip.addr == 192.67.34.26 && (tcp.port == 62503 or tcp.port == 17633)

No.	Time	Source	Destination	Protocol	Length	Info
1	2020-06-21 16:18:17.562484	1.1.2.2	192.67.34.26	TCP	66	62503 → 443 [SYN] Seq
3	2020-06-21 16:18:17.610750	192.67.34.26	10.0.0.202	TCP	66	443 → 17633 [SYN, ACK
4	2020-06-21 16:18:17.611271	1.1.2.2	192.67.34.26	TCP	54	62503 → 443 [ACK] Seq
5	2020-06-21 16:18:17.611719	1.1.2.2	192.67.34.26	TLSv1	571	Client Hello
9	2020-06-21 16:18:17.660308	192.67.34.26	10.0.0.202	TCP	54	443 → 17633 [RST, ACK
10	2020-06-21 16:18:17.660783	1.1.2.2	192.67.34.26	TCP	54	62503 → 443 [ACK] Seq
11	2020-06-21 16:18:17.661064	1.1.2.2	192.67.34.26	TCP	54	62503 → 443 [FIN, ACK
17	2020-06-21 16:18:17.705634	192.67.34.26	10.0.0.202	TCP	54	443 → 17633 [RST] Seq

Transmit stage packet capture

No.	Time	Source	Destination	Protocol	Length	Info
1	2020-06-21 16:18:17.563154	10.0.0.202	192.67.34.26	TCP	66	17633 → 443 [SYN] Sec
3	2020-06-21 16:18:17.611083	192.67.34.26	1.1.2.2	TCP	66	443 → 62503 [SYN, ACK
4	2020-06-21 16:18:17.611483	10.0.0.202	192.67.34.26	TCP	54	17633 → 443 [ACK] Sec
5	2020-06-21 16:18:17.612333	10.0.0.202	192.67.34.26	TLSv1	201	Client Hello
9	2020-06-21 16:18:17.660460	10.0.0.202	192.67.34.26	TCP	54	17633 → 443 [FIN, ACK
10	2020-06-21 16:18:17.660562	192.67.34.26	1.1.2.2	TCP	54	443 → 62503 [FIN, ACK
11	2020-06-21 16:18:17.661187	192.67.34.26	1.1.2.2	TCP	54	443 → 62503 [ACK] Sec

Filter: ip.addr == 192.67.34.26 && (tcp.port == 62503 or tcp.port == 17633)

Following the packet capture stages above, from the firewall perspective, the client hello went out, and that was it. Thankfully, the receive and transmit stages show much more. The names of these stages lend a hint to what you'll see in the capture. In the receive stage, this is everything received by the firewall interface. You see the SYN from the client to the web server, but you then see a SYN/ACK from the server to the global NAT address. This is what was received. If you cross-reference this with the transmit capture, you'll see the SYN/ACK from the webserver to the actual client IP address. The real key here, however, is in the receive capture. There are RST packets from the server to the global NAT address. This is the point at which the server realized it could not negotiate a usable cipher suite, so it reset the connection.

Lastly, I'll return to the Decryption Profile and enable "SHA1". Then, I'll browse to https://www.yellowknife.ca and perform a packet capture, in the receive stage, to show that the webserver is now responding with a "Server Hello" versus sending an RST flagged packet.

| 277 | 2020-06-22 13:00:21.248812 | 192.67.34.26 | 10.0.0.202 | TLSv1.2 | 581 | Server Hello, |
| 278 | 2020-06-22 13:00:21.252905 | 192.67.34.26 | 10.0.0.202 | TLSv1.2 | 581 | Server Hello |

Frame (581 bytes) | Reassembled TCP (3447 bytes)

Cipher Suite: TLS_ECDHE_RSA_WITH_AES_256_CBC_SHA (0xc014)

As you can see, the webserver is negotiating with the SHA1 authentication algorithm, and we're back in business.

In addition to setting the protocol and algorithms you desire, you can also block traffic that is using unsupported cipher suites. If you don't explicitly block it, the firewall will add the server to the exclude cache for twelve hours (43,200 seconds). You can view these entries in the CLI using the command string "show system setting ssl-decrypt exclude-cache".

```
jbworley79@PA-220> show system setting ssl-decrypt exclude-cache

VSYS   SERVER                    APP              TIMEOUT  REASON
CH


jbworley79@PA-220> []
```

I had an interesting experience with unsupported cipher suites. It was noted by the Net-D department that a specific website was not being decrypted when it should have been. I investigated further and found that the webserver was using elliptic curve cryptography. Our Pan-OS version at the time was not capable of handling this request, so it would exclude the server and not decrypt the flow. If I had updated our Decryption Profile to block unsupported cipher suites, the firewall would have denied the connection.

Alright, that wraps up this chapter on Forward Proxy Decryption. To recap, we enabled the certificate for Forward Proxy Trust, then we configured a decryption policy to decrypt our Internet-bound traffic, and lastly, we created and applied a Decryption Profile to explicitly allow our choice of TLS protocol and key exchange, encryption, and authentication algorithms. I hope you can see that the configuration options are quite vast, providing you with a good deal of flexibility in configuring "break and inspect" for your network. Now, it's time to look a little deeper and match on some URLs

Chapter 6: Categories and External Dynamic Lists (EDL)

So, you want to match URLs? Let's look at that question a little bit further. So, what is a URL? URL stands for uniform resource locator. In most circles, this is used to reference the protocol, say hypertext transfer protocol secure (HTTPS), and the domain name of the resource, say www.google.com. With that description, we can assume that the URL is https://www.google.com. The term "URL" tends to be used loosely to describe anything you type into the address bar of a web browser. The actual term we're after is Uniform Resource Identifier (URI), as described in RFC-3986 - Uniform Resource Identifier (URI): Generic Syntax (https://tools.ietf.org/html/rfc3986#page-22). This document goes into detail describing the individual components of a URI. For our purposes, I will provide a separate outline to describe the components and how they're seen within the firewall.

Here is an example "fictitious" URI:
https://www.google.com/users/checkID?name_info

The individual components of this URI are as follows:
"https://":   protocol
"www.google.com":   the domain name
"/user/checkID":   path (first forward slash after domain name)
"?name_info":   parameter (uses "?" to signal the start of a query string)

According to Palo Alto Networks, each element of information is a token, and these individual elements are divided up using "token separators". For the URI above, the elements are: "www", "google", "com", "users", "checkID", "name_info"

Palo Alto Networks identifies the following characters as token separators: ("." "/" "?" "&" "=" ";" "+"). Per the URI listed above, the separators being used are: ("." "/" "?").

If you're confused by all these characters and terms, don't worry. It will become clear when we start adding entries into custom URL categories and EDLs.

There is another component to this I want to touch on. For the URI example I provided, the firewall can match this URI entirely if decryption is taking place. Any element besides the domain name is only visible within the HTTP/HTTP2 protocol communication, which is tunneled inside of HTTPS. If the firewall does not decrypt the flow, it will only see certificate common name and server name indication (SNI) info in the initial TLS handshake. So, to sum up all of the available options for matching a URI based on whether or not decryption is taking place, the URI "https://www.google.com/users/checkID?name_info" can be handled in the following ways:

1. No Decrypt: can only match on www.google.com, using variations of wildcards to match against certificate common name and SNI

2. Decrypt: can also pick up protocol (HTTP application inside the tunnel) and match on path/parameter

Section 6.1: Custom URL Categories and PAN-DB

So first, we're going to work with custom URL categories. As of PAN-OS 8.1, the custom URL category limit is 500. Palo Alto Networks does install a URL category database, called PAN-DB. You can navigate to their website (https://urlfiltering.paloaltonetworks.com/) where you can test a domain name to see what category it belongs to. Also, through this website, you can request to have the category changed. Sometimes they'll do it, sometimes they won't. If its current category is "Unknown", they'll most likely accept your recommended category, assuming it's not WAY off the mark.

Additionally, for URL category testing, you can use the CLI to test. Just SSH to the box and type in "test url" plus the URL you want to test.

```
jbworley79@PA-220> test url www.httpvshttps.com

www.httpvshttps.com computer-and-internet-info low-risk (Base db) expires in 1338 seconds
www.httpvshttps.com computer-and-internet-info low-risk (Cloud db)

jbworley79@PA-220>
```

Looking at the example above, I ran a test for "httpvshttps.com". The firewall has this domain classified under the "computer-and-internet-info" category. Well, what if I set a custom URL category for it? Will it override this categorization? We'll stay with the CLI for this one. Go into edit mode by typing "configure", then input the following command string "set profiles custom-url-category httpvshttps type "URL List" list www.httpvshttps.com"

```
jbworley79@PA-220>
conjbworley79@PA-220> configure
Entering configuration mode
[edit]
jbworley79@PA-220# set profiles custom-url-category httpvshttps type "URL List" list www.httpvshttps.com

[edit]
jbworley79@PA-220# commit
```

If you wish, you can navigate to and view the new category in the GUI. Select the Objects tab at the top, then expand the Custom Objects category in the left-hand column, and lastly select the URL Category link. If you have a lot of custom categories, you can filter to locate the new category based on any information contained in the custom URL category configuration.

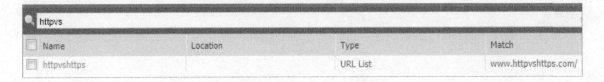

	Name	Location	Type	Match
	httpvshttps		URL List	www.httpvshttps.com/

Alright, let's run our CLI test again and see what we get.

```
jbworley79@PA-220> test url www.httpvshttps.com

www.httpvshttps.com computer-and-internet-info low-risk (Base db) expires in 880 seconds
www.httpvshttps.com computer-and-internet-info low-risk (Cloud db)

jbworley79@PA-220>
```

No dice, it's still "computer-and-internet-info". So, these tests are relying strictly on the PAN-DB database downloaded via the URL Filtering license, as well as a URL query in Palo Alto Networks' database in the cloud. Also, if you're a fan of "test security-policy-match", you cannot use custom URL categories or EDLs in these tests. You will receive a "Server error : Unrecognized category".

```
jbworley79@PA-220> test security-policy-match protocol 6 from Inside to Outside source 192.168.2.50 destination 45.33.7.16 de
stination-port 443 application ssl category httpvshttps

Server error : Unrecognized category
Error parsing arguments

jbworley79@PA-220>
```

On the other hand, if I use Palo's PAN-DB category, I get a valid result

```
jbworley79@PA-220> test security-policy-match protocol 6 from Inside to Outside source 192.168.2.50 destination 45.33.7.16 de
stination-port 443 application ssl category computer-and-internet-info

"Inside_Out; index: 10" {
        from [ Inside VPN ];
        source any;
        source-region none;
        to Outside;
        destination any;
        destination-region none;
        user any;
        category any;
        application/service 0:any/any/any/any;
        action allow;
        icmp-unreachable: no
        terminal yes;
}
```

So just know that "test url" and "test security-policy-match" rely solely on PAN-DB and will not provide proper results if you are using custom categories and EDLs.

Now, there is a way to see the local custom categorization. If you view the traffic logs for traffic to a specific URL that is contained within a custom category or EDL, you will see this category listed in the logs, PROVIDED you update your URL Filtering Profile to "alert" for the custom category or EDL. To do this, select the Objects tab at the top, then expand the Security Profiles category in the left-hand column, and lastly select the URL Filtering link. Click on the URL Filtering Profile that you are referencing in the security rule configuration (in my case,

"URL_Base"), find the new category (httpvshttps), and set the "Site Access" column to "alert". Lastly, click OK and commit the configuration.

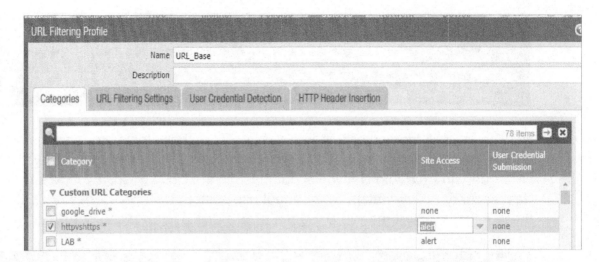

Now, when you view the actual traffic in the traffic log, you will see the custom category listed.

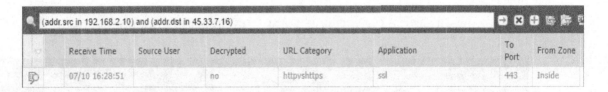

However, if you switch to the detailed log view, you'll see the custom URL category listed first, followed by the PAN-DB category.

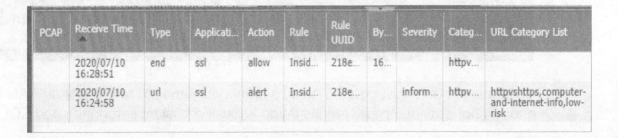

So, as you can see, there are some nuances associated with custom URL categories and how the firewall interprets them. You are, in fact, locally recategorizing the URL, knowing of course that PAN-DB is ready to handle the categorization if you remove your custom URL category or EDL entries. Custom URL Categories and EDLs are extremely powerful, in that they can be used as criteria for a policy match, and/or they can be used to act on traffic during content inspection. We will dig into these topics more in the coming sections.

I want to end this section with some tests policy matching based on custom and PAN-BD URL categories. As I showed in the last example, the firewall appears to have the custom URL category preferred, but it also still lists the PAN-DB category. If I create two policies, using a URL category as part of the policy matching criteria, and if I list the PAN-DB category in a rule above another rule listing the custom URL category, will the firewall match the PAN-DB rule?

To begin, select the Policies tab at the top, select the Security link in the left-hand column, and then click Add at the bottom of the page. I will create two policies: one matching the "computer-and-internet-info" URL category, and I will make another rule below the previous one matching the "httpvshttps" custom URL category. I have chosen to list these policies using the CLI so you can see all settings.

```
PAN-DB {
  profile-setting {
    group default;
  }
  to Outside;
  from Inside;
  source any;
  destination any;
  source-user any;
  category computer-and-internet-info;
  application any;
  service application-default;
  hip-profiles any;
  action allow;
}
```

```
"Custom URL Category" {
  profile-setting {
    group default;
  }
  to Outside;
  from Inside;
  source any;
  destination any;
  source-user any;
  category httpvshttps;
  application any;
  service application-default;
  hip-profiles any;
  action allow;
}
```

You can view rules in the CLI by typing "configure" to enter edit mode, then type "edit rulebase security rules [RULENAME]". Once you've entered edit mode for the specific rule, you can simply type "show" and you will receive output like the examples above. Now I will commit the config and test the traffic.

URL Category	To Port	From Zone	To Zone	Source	Destination	Action	Rule
httpvshttps	443	Inside	Outside	192.168.2.10	45.33.7.16	allow	PAN-DB

So, looking at the traffic log example above, even though it lists the category as "httpvshttps", it still chose the first rule in the stack since the firewall still considers this URL a member of the "computer-and-internet-info" category. So we know as a matter of matching criteria for a policy match, top-down wins, regardless of category, as long as the URL matches any specific category: custom, EDL, or PAN-DB, but what if we modify the URL Filtering Profile to block "computer-and-internet-info" and allow "httpvshttps"? To do this, select the Objects tab at the top, then expand the Security Profiles category in the left-hand column, and lastly select the URL Filtering link. Click on the URL Filtering Profile that you are referencing in the security rule configuration (in my case, "URL_Base"), search for "computer-and-internet-info" and update the "Site Access" column to "block". Once finished click OK and commit the config.

NOTE: Remember, the custom category "httpvshttps" is already set to "alert".

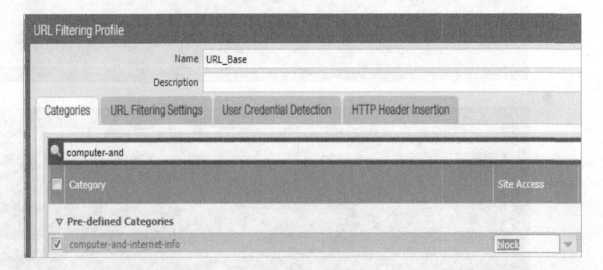

In this case, it is best to view the URL Filtering logs. Select the Monitor tab, then select the URL Filtering link in the left-hand column. In this case, I will add a filter for the source IP of my client, and a destination IP of the webserver IP for www.httpvshttps.com, ((addr.src in 192.168.2.10) and (addr.dst in 45.33.7.16)).

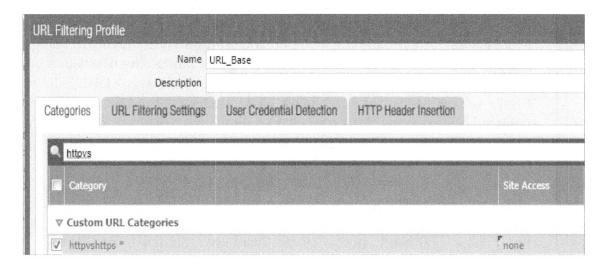

Category	App...	URL Category List	URL	Action	From Zone	To Zone
httpvshttps	ssl	httpvshttps,comput and-internet-info,low-risk	www.httpvshttps.com/	alert	Inside	Outside

As you can see, the firewall chose the "alert" setting of the "httpvshttps" category versus the "block" setting of the "computer-and-internet-info" category. Just to make sure, I'll update the "httpvshttps" setting to "none".

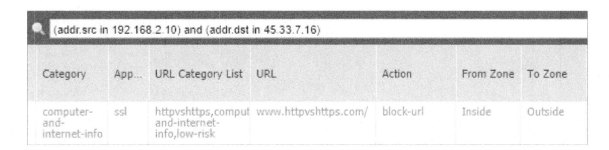

Now, looking at the logs, there you can see that we are now blocking per the "block-url" action.

Category	App...	URL Category List	URL	Action	From Zone	To Zone
computer-and-internet-info	ssl	httpvshttps,comput and-internet-info,low-risk	www.httpvshttps.com/	block-url	Inside	Outside

So, if using any type of URL category (custom, EDL, PAN-BD) as part of a policy match, whichever category is used first in a policy stack will win. On the other hand, as it relates to content inspection, custom URL categories take precedence over PAN-DB in URL Filtering Profiles.

NOTE: When you configure custom URL categories or EDLs, they, by default, are set to "none" in URL Filtering Profiles, so if you want to log traffic to these categories per the URL Filtering logs, or if you want to use them for content inspection, you'll have to update your profiles accordingly. Also, categories with a setting of "allow" do not log either, so you should always set "allow" categories to "alert".

As a general rule, I keep a URL Filtering Profile handy were I set all categories to "alert", and any time I add a new custom category, I modify the profile to set all categories to "alert". Why? When I create a custom category, I'm generally doing so to add it to a policy to be used as matching criteria. Also, I want to see the URL Filtering logs for this traffic since it significantly aids in research and troubleshooting. Since the policy match criteria are specific to a custom URL category, I'm not concerned with bypassing content inspection and letting through unwanted traffic: it won't match the policy, so it doesn't matter. There is a slight issue, however, that might catch you off-guard and make you think you've made a horrible mistake. The traffic log will show hits on the rule with a custom URL category set as matching criteria, in addition to having a URL Filtering Profile with all categories set to allow. Rest assured, if the URL doesn't match the custom URL category of the rule, and you have URL Filtering Profiles associated with lower policies that block that specific URL and/or category, it is being blocked. I'll provide a quick example.

I have two URL Filtering Profiles displayed below: "URL_Base" and "Alert_All". As you can see, "Alert_All" has 78 categories set to "alert", while "URL_Base" has 2 "allow", 69 "alert", and 4 "block". Also, note that "URL_Base" has "computer-and-internet-info" set to block still.

URL_Base		Allow Categories (2)	Allow Categories (
		Alert Categories (69)	Alert Categories ((
		Continue Categories (0)	Continue Categori
		Block Categories (4)	Block Categories (
		Override Categories (0)	
Alert_All		Allow Categories (0)	Allow Categories (
		Alert Categories (78)	Alert Categories ((
		Continue Categories (0)	Continue Categori
		Block Categories (0)	Block Categories (
		Override Categories (0)	

I will also make two policies:

1. The top policy "Custom_URL_Category" allows any IP, any application (service application-default), to custom URL category "httpvshttps" with the "Alert_All" URL Filtering Profile set

2. The bottom policy "All_Others" allows any IP, any application (service application-default), any URL category, with the "URL_Base" URL Filtering Profile set

```
Custom_URL_Category {
  profile-setting {
    profiles {
      url-filtering Alert_All;
    }
  }
  to Outside;
  from Inside;
  source any;
  destination any;
  source-user any;
  category httpvshttps;
  application any;
  service application-default;
  hip-profiles any;
  action allow;
}
```

```
All_Others {
  profile-setting {
    group default;
  }
  to Outside;
  from Inside;
  source any;
  destination any;
  source-user any;
  category any;
  application any;
  service application-default;
  hip-profiles any;
  action allow;
}
```

As a test, I will first browse to http://www.httpvshttps.com, then I will browse to http://www.pcmag.com (this site falls under the "computer-and-internet-info" category). I will first use the URL Filtering logs with the following filter

(addr.src in 192.168.2.10) and ((addr.dst in 45.33.7.16) or (addr.dst in 104.17.0.0/16))

NOTE: www.pcmag.com resolution provided two IP addresses (104.17.101.99 and 104.17.142.99), so I'm using a simple "supernet" match, which should be fine

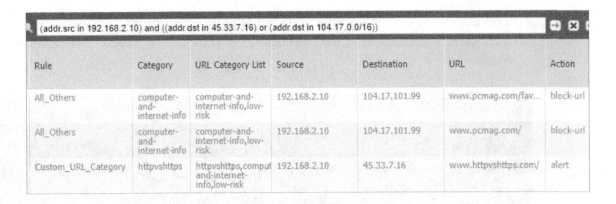

Rule	Category	URL Category List	Source	Destination	URL	Action
All_Others	computer-and-internet-info	computer-and-internet-info,low-risk	192.168.2.10	104.17.101.99	www.pcmag.com/fav...	block-url
All_Others	computer-and-internet-info	computer-and-internet-info,low-risk	192.168.2.10	104.17.101.99	www.pcmag.com/	block-url
Custom_URL_Category	httpvshttps	httpvshttps,comput and-internet-info,low-risk	192.168.2.10	45.33.7.16	www.httpvshttps.com/	alert

As you can see, the firewall reports the proper rule names and actions taken: allow www.httpvshttps.com and block www.pcmag.com. Perfect, now let's look at the traffic log using the following filter: (rule eq Custom_URL_Category)

Since this rule is set to match on www.httpvshttps.com, we should only see a log for traffic to 45.33.7.16, right?

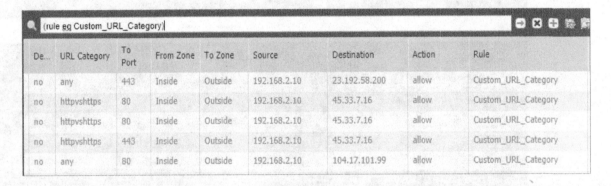

De...	URL Category	To Port	From Zone	To Zone	Source	Destination	Action	Rule
no	any	443	Inside	Outside	192.168.2.10	23.192.58.200	allow	Custom_URL_Category
no	httpvshttps	80	Inside	Outside	192.168.2.10	45.33.7.16	allow	Custom_URL_Category
no	httpvshttps	80	Inside	Outside	192.168.2.10	45.33.7.16	allow	Custom_URL_Category
no	httpvshttps	443	Inside	Outside	192.168.2.10	45.33.7.16	allow	Custom_URL_Category
no	any	80	Inside	Outside	192.168.2.10	104.17.101.99	allow	Custom_URL_Category

WRONG. In fact, in the traffic log, I have no logs for the filter (rule eq All_Others). We did see it block, right? Why is it logging for a rule that it can't possibly match? This is a very interesting behavior, and if you had the pleasure of configuring this and seeing the logs for the first time, I'm sure you can recall the blood rushing from your upper body as you frantically tried to figure out what was going on. Don't worry, it is blocked.

For SSL connections, you get a different response.

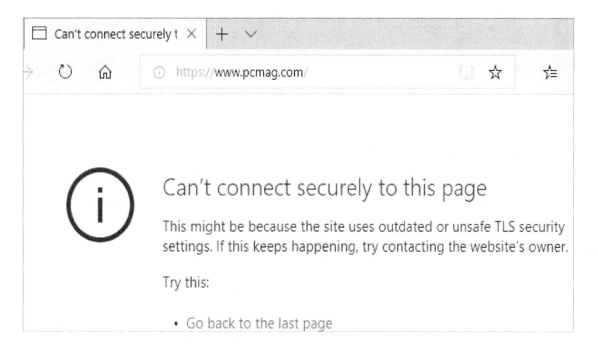

The firewall injects a TCP reset immediately after the client sends the TLS client hello.

103 3.870647	192.168.2.10	104.17.142.99	TLSv1.2	256 Client Hello	
104 3.871834	104.17.142.99	192.168.2.10	TCP	60 443 → 52343 [RST,	
105 3.872199	192.168.2.10	104.17.142.99	TCP	66 52344 → 443 [SYN]	
106 3.890423	104.17.142.99	192.168.2.10	TCP	66 443 → 52344 [SYN,	
107 3.890474	192.168.2.10	104.17.142.99	TCP	54 52344 → 443 [ACK]	
108 3.890744	192.168.2.10	104.17.142.99	TLSv1	190 Client Hello	
109 3.891886	104.17.142.99	192.168.2.10	TCP	60 443 → 52344 [RST,	

In the case of response pages, the firewall sends these via HTTP, and since it is not capable of establishing a secure TLS connection to deliver the response page, it simply resets the connection. For the HTTP traffic, the firewall provides a 503 (Service Unavailable), and the webpage text shows "Web Page Blocked…".

102 2.008666	192.168.2.10	104.17.142.99	TCP	66 52391 → 80 [SYN] Seq=0 Win=65535
103 2.026187	104.17.142.99	192.168.2.10	TCP	66 80 → 52391 [SYN, ACK] Seq=0 Ack=1
104 2.026291	192.168.2.10	104.17.142.99	TCP	54 52391 → 80 [ACK] Seq=1 Ack=1 Win=
105 2.026460	192.168.2.10	104.17.142.99	HTTP	419 GET / HTTP/1.1
106 2.028170	104.17.142.99	192.168.2.10	HTTP	1300 HTTP/1.1 503 Service Unavailable

106 2.028170	104.17.142.99	192.168.2.10	HTTP	1300 HTTP/1.1 503 Service Unavailable (text/html)
107 2.028174	104.17.142.99	192.168.2.10	TCP	60 80 → 52391 [FIN, ACK] Seq=1247 Ack=1 Win=1048

```
<body bgcolor="#e7e8e9">\r\n
<div id="content">\r\n
<h1>Web Page Blocked</h1>\r\n
<p>Access to the web page you were trying to visit has been blocked in accordance with company policy. Please contact
```

Alright, I think we've covered enough of the intricacies of custom URL categories and PAN-DB and how they interact and work together. Now, let's configure a URL category to match TLS traffic.

Section 6.2: Custom URL Categories for TLS

There are two ways for the firewall to establish a URL category match for TLS traffic:

- Match using SNI information in the client hello
- Match using server certificate subject information when the server delivers it

First, I want to provide an example of the last option. Browsers are configured to send SNI info in the client hello packet, and although new updates are coming out that enable administrators to encrypt the SNI information, there doesn't appear to be a way to disable the use of SNI outright. Therefore, to show an example of matching on certificate information using a custom URL category, I'm going to use LDAP over SSL to prove the point. This flow, at least when using a Palo firewall, does not include SNI information in the client hello.

I have an LDAP profile configured on my Palo firewall, which connects to my Active Directory server. I have triggered a few LDAP lookups while running a packet capture, so I'll use this traffic as an example of the firewall making a URL category match based on the server certificate subject information.

If you look at the packet capture example, you'll see the client hello being transmitted, over TCP-636, without the server name extension.

```
     35 321.265646      192.168.168.2          192.168.128.10         TLSv1.2      361 Client Hello
     36 331 373105       103 168 138 10         103 168 168 3          TCD         1514 636 . 46300
Transmission Control Protocol, Src Port: 46299, Dst Port: 636, Seq: 1, Ack: 1, Len: 307
Transport Layer Security
 ∨ TLSv1.2 Record Layer: Handshake Protocol: Client Hello
      Content Type: Handshake (22)
      Version: TLS 1.0 (0x0301)
      Length: 302
   ∨ Handshake Protocol: Client Hello
         Handshake Type: Client Hello (1)
         Length: 298
         Version: TLS 1.2 (0x0303)
       > Random: 5f0cf357d6bfca286f1aff232f232bb9ff92a77b6e8dce95…
         Session ID Length: 0
         Cipher Suites Length: 148
       > Cipher Suites (74 suites)
         Compression Methods Length: 1
       > Compression Methods (1 method)
         Extensions Length: 109
       > Extension: ec_point_formats (len=4)
       > Extension: supported_groups (len=52)
       > Extension: session_ticket (len=0)
       > Extension: signature_algorithms (len=32)
       > Extension: heartbeat (len=1)
```

The server then responds with the server hello and attaches a certificate. You can see the common name "AD.lab.com" listed.

```
 .273304      192.168.128.10         192.168.168.2          TLSv1.2      535 Server Hello, Certificate,
  274133      103 168 168 3          103 168 138 10         TCD          54 46300 . 636 [ACK] Seq=308 A
on Control Protocol, Src Port: 636, Dst Port: 46299, Seq: 1461, Ack: 308, Len: 481
bled TCP Segments (1941 bytes): #36(1460), #37(481)]
Layer Security
 Record Layer: Handshake Protocol: Multiple Handshake Messages
ent Type: Handshake (22)
ion: TLS 1.2 (0x0303)
th: 1936
shake Protocol: Server Hello
shake Protocol: Certificate
andshake Type: Certificate (11)
ength: 1452
ertificates Length: 1449
ertificates (1449 bytes)
  Certificate Length: 1446
  Certificate: 308205a23082048aa00302010202137c00000002c5455cbd… (id-at-commonName=AD.lab.com)
```

So, based on the certificate common name, I'm going to create a new Custom URL Category to match it. To do this, select the Objects tab at the top, click on and expand the Custom Objects section in the left-hand column, and lastly select the URL Category link. In this case, I'm going to create a new category called "wildcard.lab.com_CATEGORY", set the type to "URL List", and add in URL "AD.lab.com/". Of course, once finished, click OK and commit the config.

Now, if you're following along and using LDAP over SSL within the firewall for this test, select the Device tab, select the User Identification link in the left-hand column, select the "Group Mapping Settings" tab in the main page section and click on your configured Group Mapping to open the configuration page. Once it opens, select the "Group Include List" tab. You should see the LDAP tree, per your configured LDAP server profile, under "Available Groups". Click the arrow to the left of the group to expand. If LDAP queries are working, the group should populate with all containers within the tree.

And with that, we have generated the LDAP TCP-636 traffic. Now, select the Monitor tab at the top, expand the Logs section in the left-hand column, and select the Traffic link. Once the page loads, input a filter using (port.dst eq 636). As you can see in the example below, we have a match of the traffic per the custom URL category, and this is solely based on the server "certificate" response, in which the firewall establishes a match of the certificate subject name (common name) to a custom URL category.

(port.dst eq 636)						
URL Category	To Port	From Zone	To Zone	Source	Destination	Action
wildcard.lab.com_CATEGORY	636	Inside	Farm	192.168.168.2	192.168.128.10	allow

Alright, so this brings up a great question: which match will take priority? For instance, if I have a URL category that matches the SNI field in a client hello, but I also have a URL category that will match the certificate subject, which one will the firewall use? Let's go ahead and test this.

If using Windows, you can open your "hosts" file under "C:\Windows\System32\drivers\etc" and input an IP to name entry to enforce browsing to a resource using a name different than the public DNS name of the site. Alright, that might sound a little confusing. To clarify, in my case I'm performing test connections to my webserver (web.lab.com – 192.168.128.30). This name is a DNS-configured name for this site, and the certificate that it provides in response to a connection includes the common name "web.lab.com" and subject alternative names for DNS listed as "web.lab.com" and IP listed as "192.168.128.30". I'm going to try and force URL category verification by inputting an IP-to-name mapping in my "hosts" file using the following example.

```
# localhost name resolution is handled within DNS itself.
#       127.0.0.1       localhost
#       ::1             localhost
192.168.128.30      www.snimatch.com
```

So, with this configuration, I will browse to https://www.snimatch.com/test/test.txt and see how the firewall categorizes the URL.

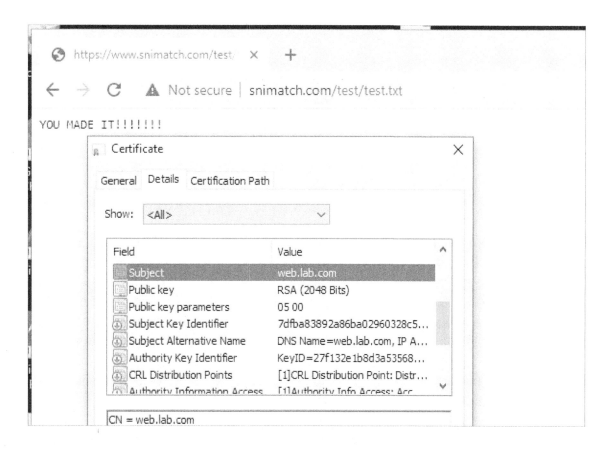

As you can see, the subject (CN) is "web.lab.com", even though I browsed this site using www.snimatch.com. You can also see that it did not establish a secure connection, in that the SNI from the client did not match the contents of the certificate, for obvious reasons. I am also including an example of the subject alternative names below so you can see what this looks like.

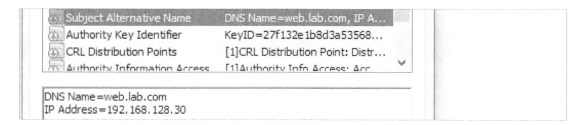

Ok, so let's check the firewall and see what logged. We will check both the Traffic and URL Filtering logs.

NOTE: I have all categories set to "alert" for the URL Filtering Profile I have configured in the applicable rule.

First, let's view the Traffic log.

| | 07/20 09:23:21 | no | unknown | | | 443 | Inside | Farm | 192.168.2.10 | 192.168.128.30 |

The category is listed as "unknown". This is the first clue of how the firewall interprets and prioritizes URL matching criteria. I have a custom URL category for "lab.com" and "*.lab.com", so if a certificate match was a priority, it should have listed "LAB" as the URL category. Alright, let's look at the URL Filtering logs.

| | 07/20 09:23:12 | Inside_Farm | | unknown | high-risk,unknown | 192.168.2.10 | 192.168.128.30 | www.snimatch.com/ |

Looks like it stayed with the SNI match of www.snimatch.com. So, we can safely assume that the URL categorization matching process does not persist throughout the session, and really why would it? The URL match is completed while the initial connection is established every time. Applications can shift within the same flow, but the URL will not. Of course, a web application can include references to other URLs, but those are each a separate connection of their own.

So, just know that URL categories will match per SNI information first, and in the absence of SNI, the certificate subject name will be used.

Next, I want to point out a potential security breach issue that can occur when you create a custom URL entry without adding a "/" to the end of the string. If I input an entry, say "www.snimatch.com", and browse to a site with a higher-level domain, say "www.snimatch.com.overrun", it will still match the URL category. To provide an example, I will create a new category called "overrun". Next, I will add an entry for "www.snimatch.com", and I will update my client "hosts" file to map www.snimatch.com.overrun to 192.168.128.30.

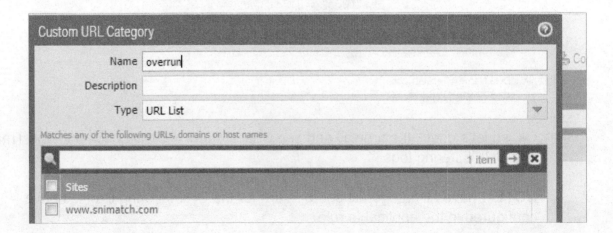

```
# localhost name resolution is handled within DNS itself.
#       127.0.0.1        localhost
#       ::1              localhost
192.168.128.30     www.snimatch.com.overrun
```

Lastly, I need to update my common URL Filtering Profile to "alert" on this category and commit the config.

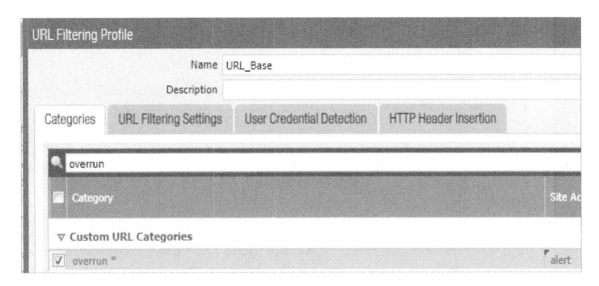

Now, I need to browse to this site and review the logs in the firewall. Specifically, I will review the URL Filtering logs to see how the firewall categorizes this URL.

As you can see, the firewall categorized "www.snimatch.com.overrun" under the "overrun" category, which only has a URL matching string of "www.snimatch.com". This can cause you to allow traffic that you did not intend to allow. For instance, what if you matched on "www.google.com" within a custom URL category to allow traffic, and your organization's security policy did not allow Internet connections from the enterprise to locations outside of the United States? Then, let's say someone internal, on an enterprise system, browsed to "www.google.com.hk". They, unwittingly, have circumvented your organizational security policy.

To fix this anomaly, add a "/" to the end of the URL string.

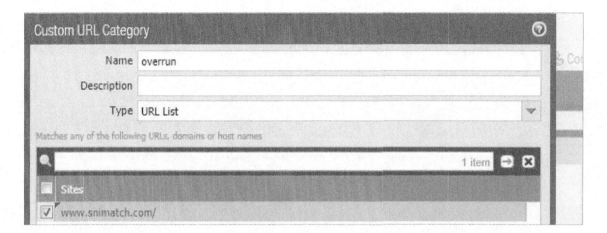

And we're back in business. I have not found any reported reason, per Palo on why this happens, but you can easily resolve this issue by making a habit of ending all domain name URL strings with a "/".

Alright, we've had quite a lot of fun working with TLS flows and custom URL categories. Just remember that when working exclusively with TLS URL category matching, only input the domain name: never include path information. Also, always end the domain string with a "/".

Ok, now we need to go deeper by looking at path and parameter information inside the TLS tunnel.

Section 6.3: Custom URL Categories for HTTP

HTTP provides a lot more possibilities for URL category matching. For instance, when I was doing test connections to https://www.snimatch.com earlier, I was including a path (/test/test.txt). This URL includes a specific resource "test.txt" that displays the text "YOU MADE IT!!!!!!". So, to prove a point, because I love proving points, I will make a URL category that matches the full URI "www.snimatch.com/test/test.txt". DON'T forget to set the URL Filtering Profile to "alert" for this category.

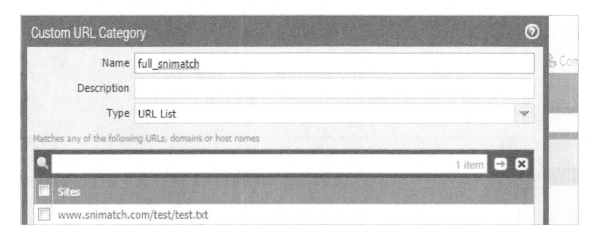

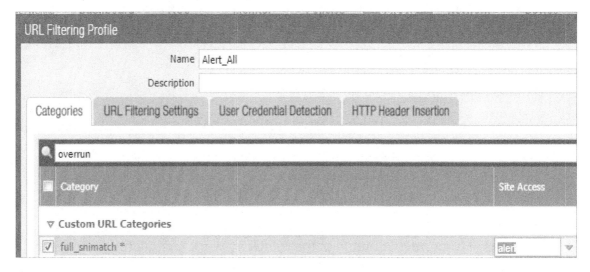

Now, if I browse to this site using TLS, what will happen?

Rule	Category	URL Category List	Source	Destination	URL
Inside_Farm	unknown	high-risk,unknown	192.168.2.10	192.168.128.30	www.snimatch.com/

Nothing happened. The URL category was recorded as "unknown", and the actual URL was recorded as "www.snimatch.com/", so there is no possibility of a match on the extended "path" information. So, what should we do? Well, we could browse to the site using HTTP versus TLS, but who would want to do that? I suppose the best course of action is to implement a decrypt policy so we can look inside. I won't go into the process of this since it was covered in an earlier chapter. I will simply create a URL category to match the SNI, and I'll implement a decrypt policy to match and decrypt the flow.

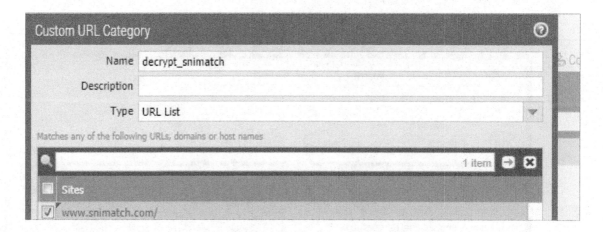

	Source			Destination				
Zone	Address	User	Zone	Address	URL Category	Service		Action
Inside	192.168.2.10	any	Farm	192.168.128.30	decrypt_snimatch	any		decrypt

Let's see what happens now.

Category	URL Category List	Source	Destination	URL	Action
full_snimatch	decrypt_snimatch,h risk,unknown	192.168.2.10	192.168.128.30	www.snimatch.com/test/test.txt	alert

Looks like we have a match of the full URL "www.snimatch.com/test/test.txt". Now, out of curiosity, what if I update the custom URL category to match "*/test/test.txt"?

Category	URL Category List	Source	Destination	URL	Action
full_snimatch	decrypt_snimatch,h risk,unknown	192.168.2.10	192.168.128.30	www.snimatch.com/test/test.txt	alert

We still have a match, as would be expected. You could also use other combinations of wildcards in between the token separators listed at the beginning of this chapter. Let's look at a query string.

If I browse to www.google.com and perform a search of "palo alto networks", what does the query info look like?

As you can see, there is a way to match this search using the string "palo+alto+networks". So how do we implement this? Well, let's divide this up into tokens. I'll list out the first eight tokens to get us through to the first search word "palo".

Token 1	Token 2	Token 3	Token 4	Token 5	Token 6	Token 7	Token 8
www	google	com	search	ei	string	q	palo

Ok, what about the token separators?

Sep 1	Sep 2	Sep 3	Sep 4	Sep 5	Sep 6	Sep 7
.	.	/	?	=	&	=

The string of characters between token separators 5 and 6 is not a good candidate to match on. I did a quick search of the Google "ei" parameter, and it is said to be a timestamp of the search per StackOverflow.com's verified Q&A message board. (https://stackoverflow.com/questions/18584386/what-does-ei-mean-in-the-google-homepage-url-https-www-google-co-in-gws-rd). So, we'll use our wildcard there.

Our URL match string should look like this:
"www.google.com/search?*=palo+alto+networks"

Just for good measure, we can also perform a packet capture on the flow to see what gets transmitted.

NOTE: Remember to use the Windows environmental variable to decrypt the flow in Wireshark, make sure you are blocking "quic" since it cannot be decrypted, and don't forget to update your decryption URL category to include www.google.com.

Now, looking at the packet capture provides an interesting find. I used a simple filter within Wireshark (http2.header.value contains "search?). Why did I use that? Well, Google begins searching for each letter you input. If you look at the example below, you'll see a string of packets that progressively spell out "palo alto networks".

Destination	Protocol	Length	Info
172.217.164.132	HTTP2	228	HEADERS[51]: GET /complete/search?q=p&cp=1&client=psy-ab&x…
172.217.164.132	HTTP2	229	HEADERS[53]: GET /complete/search?q=pa&cp=2&client=psy-ab&…
172.217.164.132	HTTP2	230	HEADERS[55]: GET /complete/search?q=pal&cp=3&client=psy-ab…
172.217.164.132	HTTP2	230	HEADERS[57]: GET /complete/search?q=palo&cp=4&client=psy-a…
172.217.164.132	HTTP2	232	HEADERS[59]: GET /complete/search?q=palo%20&cp=5&client=ps…
172.217.164.132	HTTP2	233	HEADERS[61]: GET /complete/search?q=palo%20a&cp=6&client=p…
172.217.164.132	HTTP2	234	HEADERS[63]: GET /complete/search?q=palo%20al&cp=7&client=…
172.217.164.132	HTTP2	234	HEADERS[67]: GET /complete/search?q=palo%20alt&cp=8&client…
172.217.164.132	HTTP2	235	HEADERS[69]: GET /complete/search?q=palo%20alto&cp=9&clien…
172.217.164.132	HTTP2	238	HEADERS[71]: GET /complete/search?q=palo%20alto%20&cp=10&c…

Once the user completes the search string and presses enter, a packet comes through without the "/complete/" token, and this packet replaces the URL encoding with a "+". If you reference an ASCII table, you'll find that this URL encoding (%20) refers to the hexadecimal value for a space character (0x20).

192.168.2.10	172.217.164.132	HTTP2	242 HEADERS[81]: GET /complete/sear
192.168.2.10	172.217.164.132	HTTP2	243 HEADERS[83]: GET /complete/sear
192.168.2.10	172.217.164.132	HTTP2	244 HEADERS[85]: GET /complete/sear
192.168.2.10	172.217.164.132	HTTP2	244 HEADERS[87]: GET /complete/sear
192.168.2.10	172.217.164.132	HTTP2	469 HEADERS[89]: GET /search?source
192.168.2.10	172.217.164.132	HTTP2	355 HEADERS[107]: GET /complete/co=

/search?source=hp&ei=XcUWX-rhG9PE1QH_8Yu4Dw&q=palo+alto+networks&oq=palo+alto+networks&

Alright, I have configured the URL category and I've set the URL Filtering Profile to "block" this traffic.

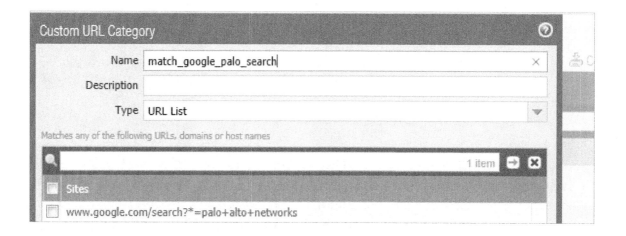

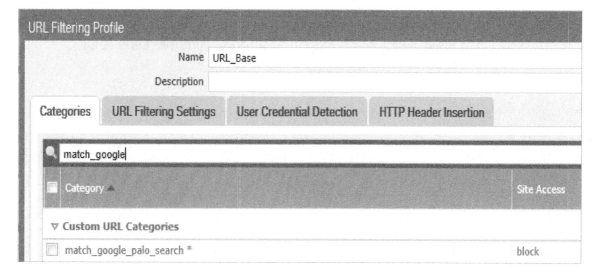

Now it's time to test this traffic. I will browse to www.google.com and enter the search string "palo alto networks" and press enter.

```
→  C    🔒 google.com/search?source=hp&ei=fdIWX6jsA5rAytMPlpC6sAg&q=palo+alto+networ
```

Web Page Blocked

Access to the web page you were trying to visit has been blocked in accordance with c
system administrator if you believe this is in error.

User: 192.168.2.10

URL: www.google.com/search?
source=hp%26ei=fdIWX6jsA5rAytMPlpC6sAg%26q=palo+alto+networks%26oq=palo-
ab

Category: match_google_palo_search

And, we're blocked. So, our URL category successfully matched on the domain, path, and parameter information in the URL string. I wouldn't use this particular configuration in a real-world scenario, but it does prove the point of how versatile URL categories can be, especially when decrypting and matching the raw HTTP information.

Now, let's have a look at configuring External Dynamic Lists (EDL).

Section 6.4: External Dynamic Lists (EDL)

EDL's provide a great advantage over custom URL categories. In short, you configure a simple web server, and you reference text documents, which list either IPs, URLs, or domains. The max number of entries is dictated by the platform you are using. You can reference https://docs.paloaltonetworks.com/pan-os/9-0/pan-os-admin/policy/use-an-external-dynamic-list-in-policy/external-dynamic-list.html to find out the maximum number for your specific platform. In my lab, I'm using a PA-220, so I can have a total of 50,000 IP, URL, domain entries each, divided among a total of 30 EDLs.

So, why use EDLs? Well, once you configure the reference point, and you reference your EDLs in rules and content inspection, there is no other configuration needed on the firewall. You simply update the text document on your web server, and the firewall downloads and updates accordingly.

URL EDLs function the same as our previously discussed custom URL categories. Domain EDLs, however, have a very specific purpose: DNS sinkhole.

For this book, I'm not going to take a deep dive into sink holing, but in general terms, DNS sink holing allows you to assign a domain EDL to a spyware profile, whereby you can identify potentially malicious domains, and you can then intercept DNS requests and have the firewall answer with a specific IP that will drop the traffic when the client tries to connect. You could set up a connection point to allow the client to connect and possibly gather some forensic data on what the client is trying to do if you wanted to.

IP EDLs serve a specific purpose as well. You assign them as IP source or destination objects in various policies depending on your needs. This is very beneficial for IP blocklists, where there is clear evidence that specific IPs have participated in sustained malicious activity, you want to block all traffic to these outright. Then, as new malicious IPs are identified, or currently blocked IPs are deemed to be benign, you can easily modify the list to support your specific needs.

Alright, to begin, first, we need to configure a simple web server that will host our text documents. Since this book is centered around Windows, we'll be using: you guessed it, Internet Information Services (IIS).

Setting up this type of web server is very simple. Once you have the IIS role added, open up the start menu and search for (type in) IIS. The IIS Manager will display, and then you can simply click on it to open.

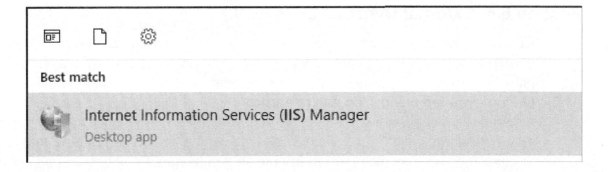

Once the IIS Manager opens, you can expand the tree in the left-hand column by clicking on the server name and then "Sites". In my case, my server name is "WEB". Once this opens, you see a site that has been preconfigured "Default Web Site". This site, in particular, is using TCP-80 (HTTP).

For our purposes, we want to encrypt the traffic, so we'll be setting up a new site with binding to TCP-443, and we'll complete the configuration to enable SSL. To begin, first right-click the "Sites" directory in the left-hand column and click "Add Website".

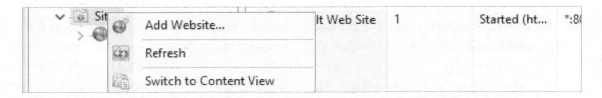

When the "Add Website" configuration page opens, you'll need to configure the following settings:

NOTE: I'll fill in the settings I'll be using for my specific configuration
Site name: EDL
Physical path: C:\EDL
Type: https
SSL certificate: web

That's it, you can leave the other settings at their default value. Once you're ready, click OK and the site will be created and started automatically.

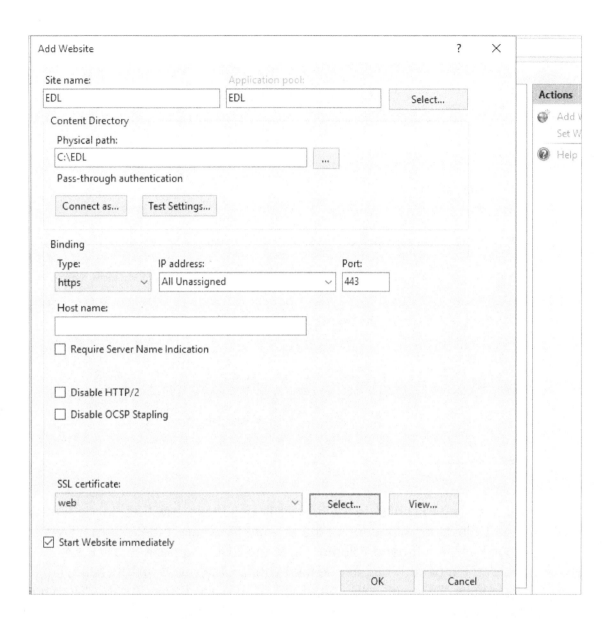

Next, you'll need to configure three text documents within the directory you chose for the new website. In this case, I'll create the following and add in some specific entries.

- Domain.txt (contains www.google.com)
- URL.txt (contains www.google.com/search?*=palo+alto+networks)
- IP.txt (contains "192.168.128.40")

Alright, once the text documents are created in the new directory on the webserver, move to your client, and try to browse to/open these documents using your web browser. If using the method I described above, you'll need to input https://#YOURSERVERNAME#/#EDL_NAME#.txt.

https://web.lab.com/domain.txt

https://web.lab.com/url.txt
https://web.lab.com/ip.txt

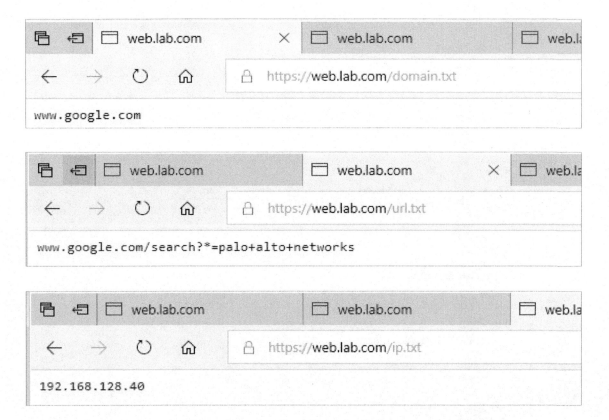

Now, we need to configure the firewall to use these new lists. In the firewall, click on the Objects tab at the top of the screen, then select the External Dynamic Lists link in the left-hand column. Once the EDL page opens, click Add at the bottom of the page. You need to give your EDL a name. In this case, I'm simply going to use "Domain", "URL", and "IP". I'll provide figures for the "Domain" list. After you enter the list name, select the type (in this case, "Domain List"), input the URL in the Source field, and lastly select the update frequency (in this case, I'll leave the default of "Hourly"). After you've entered the information, commit the configuration.

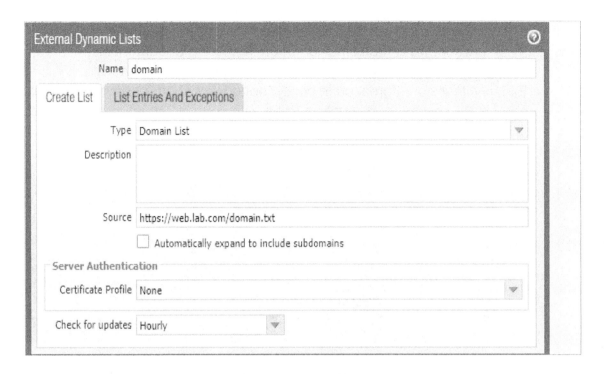

Now, you'll want to make sure that the firewall can reach these lists. To do this, once the commit completes, open up the EDL again and click "Test Source URL" at the bottom of the configuration box.

It will take a minute, but you should get a response confirming that the URL is accessible.

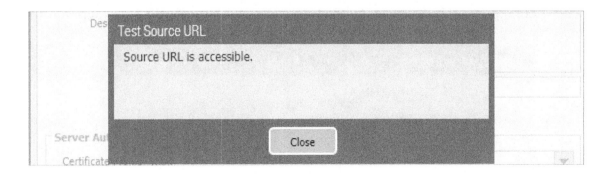

Now, move over to the firewall CLI and run the following command:

request system external-list show type domain name #LISTNAME#

You'll notice that the entries are not showing up. Why? This is part of the way EDLs function. If you don't include them in policies or content inspection, the firewall will disregard them, and as part of the response in the CLI, it will state "EDL is either not referenced in policy, not downloaded, or empty". So, just know that this is expected and is not an issue with your EDL configuration up to this point.

```
jbworley79@PA-220> request system external-list show type domain name domain

        ^ == exact match
        * == wildcard
domain

        EDL is either not referenced in policy, not downloaded, or empty

        Total valid entries     : 0
        Total ignored entries   : 0
        Total invalid entries   : 0
        Total displayed entries : 0
```

Alright, so to show the functionality of EDLs, we need to use them in policies and content inspection. Just to provide a quick example of the "domain" EDL usage, I will quickly set up a sinkhole configuration within my current spyware profile.

NOTE: Make sure you verify your security policies and identify the specific policy that will match traffic for your client's DNS requests, then identify the configured Spyware Profile and update that profile.

To begin configuration, click on the Objects tab at the top, select to expand the Security Profiles section in the left-hand column, and lastly click on the Anti-Spyware link. Then, select the Spyware Profile you wish to update. Once the configuration box opens, select the "DNS Signatures" tab at the top of the box.

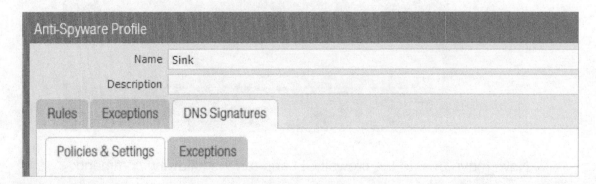

Under Policies and Settings, click Add, select your EDL domain list for the DNS Signature Source, select "sinkhole" for Action on DNS Queries, enable Packet Capture (single or extended) if you wish, and make a note of the sinkhole IPv4

setting (it's using Palo's sinkhole "sinkhole.paloaltonetworks.com"). Once finished, click OK and commit the configuration.

NOTE: All configurations in this book are IPv4-based. Please refer to online documentation for IPv6 configurations.

Now, return to the CLI, and perform a manual refresh of the EDL by typing:

refresh system external-list refresh type domain name #LIST_NAME#

```
jbworley79@PA-220> request system external-list refresh type domain name domain

EDL refresh job enqueued
jbworley79@PA-220>
```

You can check the status of the job by issuing the "show jobs all" command.

```
jbworley79@PA-220> show jobs all

Enqueued              Dequeued            ID  PositionInQ
    Type                          Status Result Completed
-----------------------------------------------------------------
-----------------------------------------------------------------
2020/07/26 11:38:45   11:38:45        8715
  EDLRefresh                          FIN    OK 11:39:46
```

So, according to the "show jobs all" output, the refresh has completed. So now, let's show the EDL again and see what we find.

```
jbworley79@PA-220> request system external-list show type domain name domain

      ^ == exact match
      * == wildcard
domain
      Total valid entries    : 1
      Total ignored entries  : 0
      Total invalid entries  : 0
      Total displayed entries : 1
      Valid domains:
            www.google.com
```

And we have a winner. We have 1 total valid entry and 1 displayed entry www.google.com. Now, to verify the sinkhole action, we need to resolve for www.google.com and observe the result.

From your client, open the command prompt and perform a name lookup (nslookup) for www.google.com. To see the appropriate record type, input "nslookup", hit Enter, then type in "set type=cname", press Enter, then lastly type in www.google.com.

```
C:\Users\west>nslookup
Default Server:  AD.lab.com
Address:  192.168.128.10

> set type=cname
> www.google.com
Server:  AD.lab.com
Address:  192.168.128.10

Non-authoritative answer:
www.google.com  canonical name = sinkhole.paloaltonetworks.com
```

As you can see, www.google.com now resolves to CNAME sinkhole.paloaltonetworks.com. If we look in the firewall threat logs, we will see full details of this lookup and the action the firewall took to deny the traffic. To view these logs, select the Monitor tab at the top, then select the Threat link in the left-hand column. If you have a lot of threat logs, just filter using your client IP as the source address.

Name	From Zone	To Zone	Source address	Destination address	To Port	A...	Action	Severity	URL
Suspicious Domain	Inside	Farm	192.168.2.10	192.168.128.10	53	dns	sinkhole	medium	Suspicious DNS ...

Per the threat logs, a suspicious domain request was recorded from 192.168.2.10, and the ultimate action taken was "sinkhole". If you open the detailed log view, you will see the actual domain name that was requested (www.google.com).

Also, remember when I configured the Spyware Profile, I selected "Extended" type for packet captures. If you look at the summary log page, you'll see a green arrow near the beginning of the left side of the log entry, facing down. Click this arrow to open the packet capture taken by the firewall. You can see from the figure below, this appears to be a snippet of the "query" packet from the client to the DNS server, and it is asking for www.google.com.

```
Packet Capture                                                                      ⊙
11:54:10.000000 00:1e:49:e8:94:42 > 08:30:6b:83:bc:11, ethertype IPv4 (0x0800), length 74: (tos 0x0
    192.168.2.10.57473 > 192.168.128.10.53: 3+ ANY? www.google.com. (32)
        0x0000:  0830 6b83 bc11 001e 49e8 9442 0800 4500    .0k.....I..B..E.
        0x0010:  003c 151b 0000 7e11 2431 c0a8 020a c0a8    .<.....~.$1......
        0x0020:  800a e081 0035 0028 8bd9 0003 0100 0001    .....5.(........
        0x0030:  0000 0000 0000 0377 7777 0667 6f6f 676c    .......www.googl
        0x0040:  6503 636f 6d00 00ff 0001                   e.com.....
```

Alright, enough with the sinkhole and domain EDL explanations. Let's move on to the URL EDL.

If you remember from the custom URL category section, we found that as far as the selection sequence for various matching categories:

- If the category is used as matching criteria for the policy, the first one (that is, the category used first in any policy working from top-down) will be selected

- If the category is used in content inspection (action set in URL Filtering Profile), a custom URL category will win over the PAN-DB category setting

So, how does an EDL fit into this scenario? Well, without performing any policy tests, I can say with 100% certainty that it will react the same as custom URL categories and PAN-DB entries when placed within a policy as matching criteria, but what about content inspection?

To test this scenario, I will add www.google.com to the "URL" EDL.

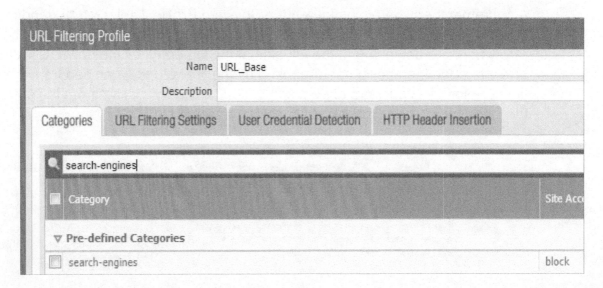

Then, I will set the PAN-DB "search-engines" category to block.

Next, I will update the "URL" EDL to alert.

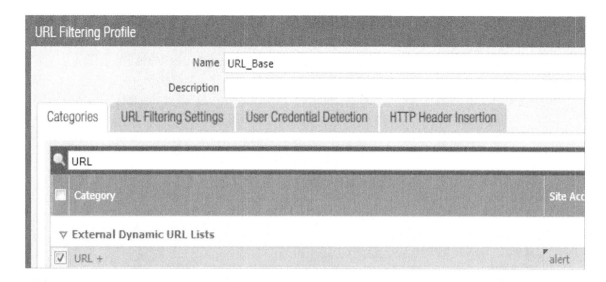

Also, in my case, I'm going to set the previous custom URL category I used "match_google_palo_search" to action "none" within the URL Filtering Profile.

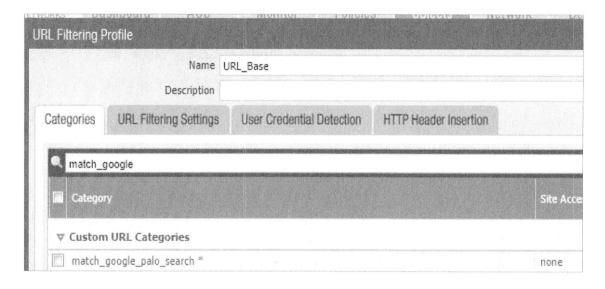

Now, if the hierarchy is correct, I should see "search-engines" listed in the domain list, but the URL category will be "URL", and my traffic will still get through.

Category	URL Category List	Source	Destination	URL	Action
URL	URL,search-engines,low-risk	192.168.2.10	172.217.2.100	www.google.com/	alert

As you can see, the URL Filtering action was "alert", and the category was listed as "URL", and the PAN-DB URL category "search-engines" is listed in the URL Category List below the EDL "URL". So, EDLs, configured for action with a URL

Filtering Profile, will override the PAN-DB action. Now, we have one more check: update the custom URL category "match_google_palo_search" to block, which will show whether or not a custom URL category overrides an EDL.

First, I will add www.google.com/ to the custom URL category.

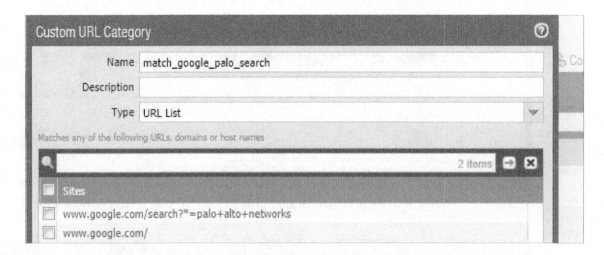

Then, I will update the URL Filtering Profile to action "block" for category "match_google_palo_search".

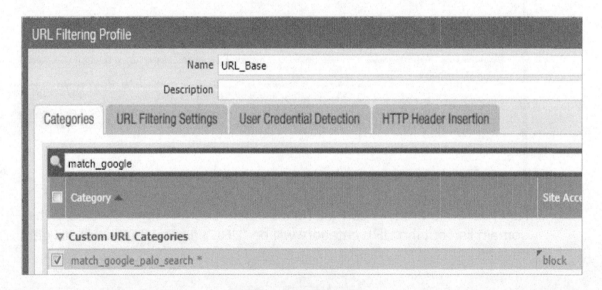

Now, it's time to test the traffic and see what happens.

Category	URL Category List	Source	Destination	URL	Action
match_google_...	URL,search-engines,low-risk	192.168.2.10	172.217.2.100	www.google.com/	block-url

As you can see, the custom URL category is the winner.

My apologies for the continued observance of this topic, but I feel that is it very important for any firewall engineer to know exactly how the firewall interprets URL matching information, whether called in a policy for matching or used to control content reachability via content inspection.

In short, using the figure below, and considering that all three listed URL categories have the same entry www.google.com, regardless of any other settings, the first rule, using the PAN-DB category "search-engines" will establish a match.

		Source		Destination		
	Name	Zone	Address	Zone	Address	URL Category
2	PAN-DB_MATCH	any	any	any	any	search-engines
3	EDL_MATCH	any	any	any	any	URL
4	CUSTOM_CAT_MATCH	any	any	any	any	match_google_p...

On the other hand, considering that all three listed URL categories have the same entry (www.google.com), when implementing a URL Filtering Profile and associating it to any of these rules listed above, custom URL category will be considered first, followed by the EDL, then lastly the Pre-defined (PAN-DB) category.

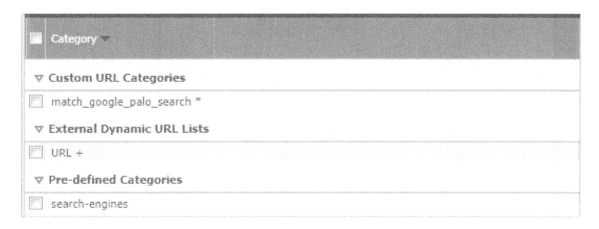

You can see that the URL Filtering Profile provides evidence of this in the way that it lists the different types of categories in hierarchical fashion top down.

Now, let's test the EDL for a match using path and parameter URI matching. We'll use the same URL we implemented in our custom URL category: www.google.com/search?*=palo+alto+networks.

NOTE: Remember, to match the information in the path and parameter fields, you must decrypt the flow.

First, I will normalize the config and undo the changes I made for the previous example. I will set the custom category "match_google_palo_search" to "none" in the URL Filtering Profile. Then, I will remove www.google.com from the URL EDL. Lastly, I will set the URL EDL and PAN-DB category "search-engines" to "alert" in the URL Filtering Profile.

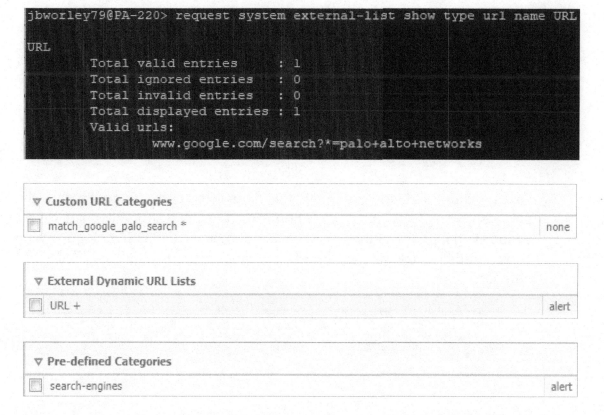

Alright, I will return to the URL Filtering logs, input the filter (url contains "palo+"), and lastly, I'll generate some browser traffic.

As you can see, the category selected was URL.

I'll wrap up this chapter with a quick configuration of the "IP" EDL. To do this, I will configure a security policy at the top of the stack, and I will list the "IP" EDL as a destination, then I will set the action to "deny".

To do this, select the Policies tab at the top of the page, then click Add at the bottom of the main page. When the Security Policy Rule configuration box opens, under the General tab, I will name it "IP_Block".

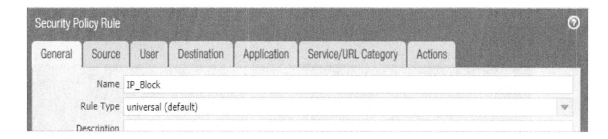

Then, under the Source tab, I will set the Source Zone and Address to "any".

Next, under the Destination tab, I will set the Destination Zone to any, and I will add the "IP" EDL as a Destination Address.

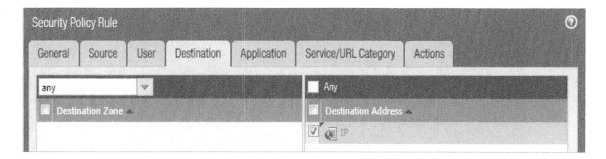

Lastly, under the Actions tab, I will set the Action to "Deny".

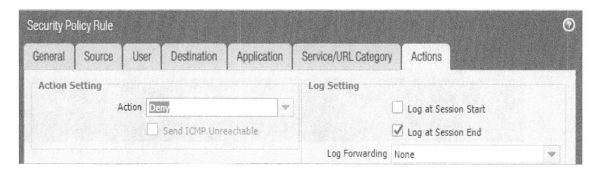

Once finished, commit the config.

Now, if you recall, before an EDL is used in any policy or content inspection, the firewall will not download it. Your CLI request to show the unused EDL will reply with "EDL is either not referenced in policy, not downloaded, or empty".

```
jbworley79@PA-220> request system external-list show type ip name IP

IP
        EDL is either not referenced in policy, not downloaded, or empty

        Total valid entries    : 1
        Total ignored entries  : 0
        Total invalid entries  : 0
        Total displayed entries : 1
        Valid ips:
                0.0.0.0/32
```

I just want to make sure you observe this since I've seen several individuals end up confused as to why an EDL they have created isn't downloading. This can cause the unsuspecting engineer to deep dive into potential web server issues, etc when in reality this is the expected behavior.

Once the commit is finished, I will issue the "refresh" CLI command, followed by the "show" command to see the results.

```
jbworley79@PA-220> request system external-list refresh type ip name IP

EDL refresh job enqueued
jbworley79@PA-220> request system external-list show type ip name IP

IP
        Total valid entries    : 1
        Total ignored entries  : 0
        Total invalid entries  : 0
        Total displayed entries : 1
        Valid ips:
                192.168.128.40
```

And we're in business. Now, I will try and ping "192.168.128.40" from my internal client, and then I'll check the Traffic logs to see the result.

```
C:\Users\west>ping 192.168.128.40

Pinging 192.168.128.40 with 32 bytes of data:
Request timed out.
```

Inside	Farm	192.168.3.100	192.168.128.40	deny	IP_Block

And, it's blocked. It's as simple as that. Domain EDLs are used in Anti-Spyware Profiles for DNS filtering, URL EDLs are used in both policies and URL Filtering Profiles, and IP EDLs are used in policies as source or destination addresses.

So, as you can see, custom URL categories and EDLs are a complex subject, but they enable you to have immense power over traffic categorization, policy matching, and content filtering. You can get lost trying out all the possibilities.

Now, we have another powerful tool at our disposal: UserID.

Chapter 7: User Identification

User ID is such a useful tool. Up to this point, we've been focusing on features to restrict or allow specific traffic for most internal users, or we've restricted the policies down to one client machine. As you can tell, these methods are quite effective, but, what if your internal users move around throughout the day: connecting to WiFi hotspots, plugging in, or connecting via VPN? How do you make sure that all of these different source address possibilities match the proper policies? Say you set up a policy to allow John to access a website from his client computer with IP address 10.10.10.10. Then, John takes his laptop home, connects via VPN, and is assigned IP address 172.16.10.10. John then calls you up and asks why he can't access the website anymore. Well, you know why, and you explain to him that his source address changed, and because of this, he cannot access the website. John doesn't care. He doesn't know anything about computers, he just needs to access the HQ payroll website. How can you make sure John can cut your paycheck on time from any IP in the enterprise? UserID.

NOTE: As with all subjects in this book, I am using a Microsoft Active Directory (AD) domain to make this configuration work.

The idea behind UserID is that for most enterprises, there is a central authentication server in use, like Microsoft AD. For AD, when a user logs into a machine the AD server generates a security log that lists two important pieces of information: the username and the IP address. With this information, the firewall can create an IP-to-user mapping so that when traffic hits the firewall from a specific IP, the firewall can cross-reference and identify the user associated with that IP. Also, you can set up an LDAP server profile, which the firewall can use to query specific security groups to find out if a user is a member of any such group. Why is this necessary? When you create policies, you can configure and match on a group versus listing each user that should be allowed or denied.

Now, for this configuration, I am going to utilize a user ID agent. The firewall will connect to the agent over TCP-5007. The user agent, which is just an application running on a Microsoft server, will use a service account to pull the security logs from AD over SMB TCP-445. Also, the user agent will poll clients directly using Windows Management Instrumentation (WMI). Alright, let's configure the agent first.

Section 7.1: Install and Configure the User-ID Agent

To begin, you need to download the UID software. If you have a Palo Alto Networks support account, you should be able to download the user agent .msi file. In my case, I have version 8.0.11 (UaInstall-8.0.11.msi). Once you have the install file downloaded to your server, click on it to install. Just click through and accept the defaults. The installation will finish quickly.

After the installation completes, click on the Windows Start menu, and type in "user-id". The application should show up as the best match.

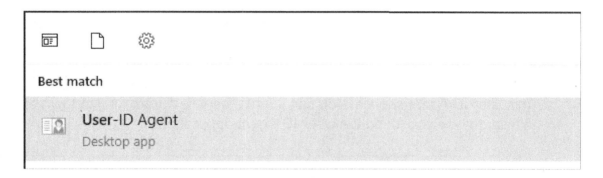

Right-Click this application, select More, then select "Run as administrator".

NOTE: You need an administrator account to install and configure the agent.

Once it opens, you'll see that the Agent Status is "running", however, there are no connected devices or connected servers. Go ahead and click "Stop" to stop the service.

To begin configuration, first and foremost, you'll need a service account in AD with the proper privileges that will allow the service to run, as well as allow the application to authenticate with AD and pull the event logs. In my case, I'm going to use an account assigned to the "Domain Admins" security group. In production, you would not do this. The service account needs to have the proper privileges to accomplish the necessary tasks, while at the same time restricting access to only those components necessary. The reason for this is that if your service account gets compromised, a malicious actor will not have the "keys to the kingdom", so to speak. Building out custom permissions in AD is beyond the scope of this book, but Palo Alto Networks covers the required account settings at https://docs.paloaltonetworks.com/pan-os/9-0/pan-os-admin/user-id/map-ip-addresses-to-users/create-a-dedicated-service-account-for-the-user-id-agent.html. Enjoy.

Alright, so the first thing we'll do, on the agent server, is open "Services" and find the User-ID Agent service. You can search "services" from the startup menu, similar to how you found the User-ID Agent application.

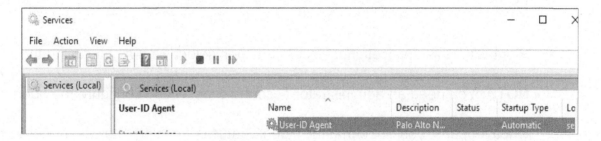

Once Services opens, and you find the User-ID Agent service, right-click, then select "Properties". Once the configuration box opens, select the "Log On" tab, under "Log on as:". Next, select "This account:", and enter the account information you acquired from your AD server. You'll need to enter the username in the user principal name (UPN) format (name@domain). Once the username is entered, type in the password twice, then click OK.

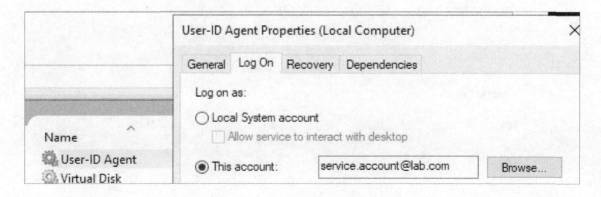

Next, return to the UID Agent configuration box. In the left-hand column, select "Setup", then click "Edit" for the Setup Configuration. Once the configuration box opens, under the Authentication tab, enter your AD account information in UPN format. Then, enter the password for the account and click OK.

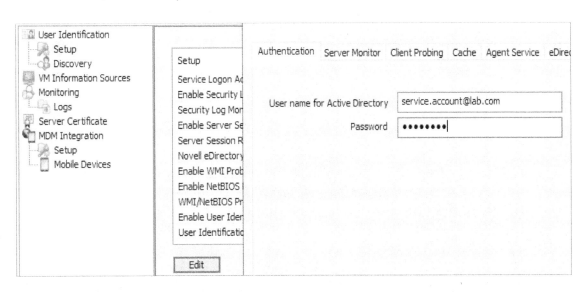

Next, select the "Discovery" link in the left-hand column. Then, under "Servers", click Add, and lastly input the details for your AD server. Once finished, click OK.

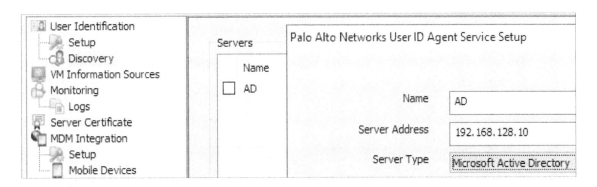

To complete the User-ID Agent configuration, in the main UID Agent window, click "Save" then "Commit". Once committed, click "Start" to start the service back up. You should see your AD server populate in the "Connected Servers" box, and the Status should show "Connected".

Connected Servers		
Server	Type	Status
AD(192.168.128.10)	Microsoft Active Directory	Connected

Alright, we now have an agent connected to AD and it should be pulling the security logs. We can verify by returning to the agent software. In the left-hand column, select "Monitoring". You should see some IP-to-user mappings, provided you have users currently authenticated in AD. In my case, I have my domain.admin@lab.com account pinned to two different IPs.

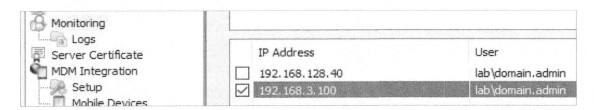

As I said before, the agent is pulling security logs from AD over SMB2 TCP-445. Let's look at the traffic and see what we find. Below is the Session Setup Request with LAB\service.account attempting to authenticate.

```
192.168.3.100    192.168.128.10    SMB2    639 Session Setup Request, NTLMSSP_AUTH, User: LAB\service.account
```

Next up, here's the Create File Request from the agent (192.168.3.100) requesting file EVENTLOG.

```
98 14.470467    192.168.3.100    192.168.128.10    SMB2    178 Ioctl Request FSCTL_QUERY_NET
99 14.470506    192.168.3.100    192.168.128.10    SMB2    194 Create Request File: EVENTLOG
100 14.471935   192.168.128.10   192.168.3.100     SMB2    326 Ioctl Response FSCTL_QUERY_NET
```

Then, the AD server responds with a Read Response (this is an aggregated packet. The total byte count in this response was 3,256, chopped up into packets below the MTU threshold of 1500 bytes).

```
148 14.498253    192.168.128.10    192.168.3.100    SMB2    478 Read Response
```

Lastly, here is the raw data from the Read Response packet showing domain.admin@LAB.COM with an IPv4 address of 192.168.128.40.

```
õðLfLeI♪c= _c= _¡♪8êMicrosoft-Windows-Security-
AuditingAD.lab.comdomain.admin@LAB.COMLAB.COMAD$S-1-5-21-2010825906-1
10000x408100000x12::ffff:192.168.128.40654050x0{a5c855b4-fc4f-474c-63
ð`LfLeI♪c= _c= _@1ZMicrosoft-Windows-Security-AuditingAD.lab.comS-1-5
1098149768-3967500490-1103domain.adminLAB0x3f701dbSeSecurityPrivilege
```

Regarding the IP-user mappings, these entries will timeout in 45 minutes, by default, if no other authentication logs are generated. You can update this value by selecting "Setup" in the left-hand column, followed by selecting "Edit" for the Setup information. Once the configuration box opens, select the "Cache" tab, and input the value, in minutes, that you wish to have entries timeout. You can set any value between 1 and 1440 (24 hours maximum). You can also disable the timeout feature by unchecking the "Enable User Identification Timeout".

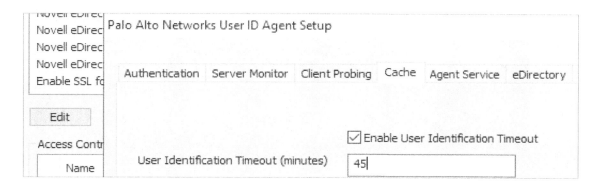

I do not suggest disabling the timeout feature. Here's a quick scenario on why. If you have a user log in and authenticate from a specific IP, they now have access, per the user ID settings within the firewall policies. If through DHCP lease renewals, or someone's deliberate action, another user gains access to that IP without any triggered AD authentication, he or she will have the same access rights as the previously authenticated user. We know, based on the previous figure of IP-to-user mappings, that a single username can be mapped to several IPs at once. I will authenticate to machine "East1.lab.com (192.168.3.2)" using domain.admin@lab.com, then I will verify the User-ID Agent logs, and lastly, I will log out domain.admin@lab.com, then log in as east1\lab (local administrator account).

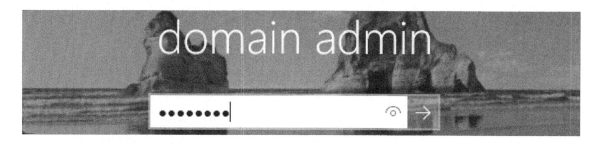

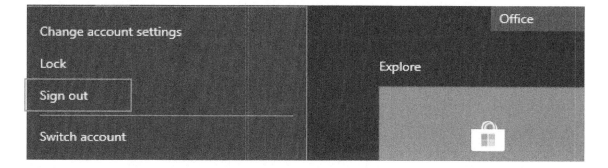

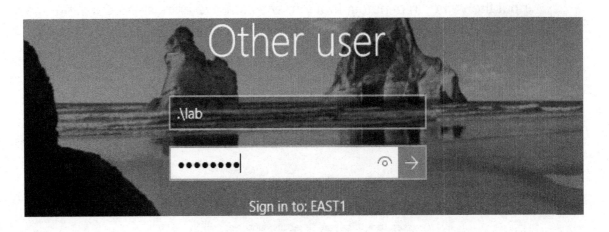

192.168.3.2	lab\domain.admin

Oh no, that's not good. Username domain.admin@lab.com has logged out, and a user has logged in with local admin account east1\lab, yet the agent still maintains the IP-to-user mapping listing LAB\domain.admin as the user for this IP, so local admin "lab" will have the same access as a domain admin per the Palo policies. This is why you want some level of timeout. If you have a domain admin jumping around, authenticating all over the enterprise doing workstation maintenance, you don't want all of those IPs to maintain domain.admin's access level forever. You can rely on Windows Management Instrumentation (WMI) probing, but it is best to make sure you have a timeout period for all entries, even if it's 45 minutes.

If I log in with a domain account to east1, the record will immediately update. In this case, I will log in with the user account east@lab.com.

192.168.3.100	lab\service.account
192.168.3.2	lab\east
192.168.178.40	lab\domain.admin

As you can see, it has updated. Also, if the entry times out and a user calls in to report a trouble that they cannot access a specific resource, double-check the IP-user-mapping. If it's missing, have them lock and unlock their computer to force a reauthentication with AD, which will generate a new security log entry and reestablish the IP-user-mapping.

Alright, so now we need to configure the Palo firewall to connect via TCP-5007 to the User-ID Agent.

Section 7.2: Configure the User-ID Agent in the Palo Firewall

There is one point of configuration we need to touch on, in the firewall, before we move forward. First, you need to enable User-ID for each Security Zone that you wish to use source user information. To do this, select the Network tab at the top, then in the left-hand column, select the Zones link. Identify each zone that you want to enable for User-ID. Then, click on each selected zone name to open the configuration box. Under the "User Identification ACL" section, check the box for "Enable User Identification". This will enable the use of User-ID information for the respective zone.

The remainder of the User Identification settings is located under the Device tab. Select this tab, and in the left-hand column, select the User ID link.

First, I want to touch on a different form of configuration outside of using the Windows Server dedicated User-ID Agent: using the built-in PAN-OS user agent. We'll configure this real quick to show how easy it is to get UserID up and running. Under the "User Mapping" tab, click on the gear icon for the "Palo Alto Networks User-ID Agent Setup" section. Once the configuration box opens, under the "Server Monitor Account" page, enter the domain username, using the down-level logon format, that has the required permissions, add the Domain's DNS Name, enter the password for your domain account, and then click OK.

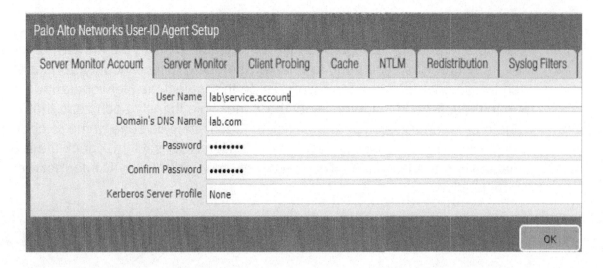

NOTE: When authenticating with Active Directory from a non-domain-joined device, there are typically two ways to enter the full username to identify the domain and user:

- Down-level logon name format: enter account name as "DOMAIN"\"USER"
- User Principle Name: enter the account name as "USER"@"DOMAIN"

Next, under the "Server Monitoring" section, click Add. Once the box opens, enter a name for your server (any name you wish), set the "Type" to "Microsoft Active Directory", set the "Transport Protocol" to WMI, and lastly, add the AD server IP address to the "Network Address" form field. Once finished, click OK, then commit the config.

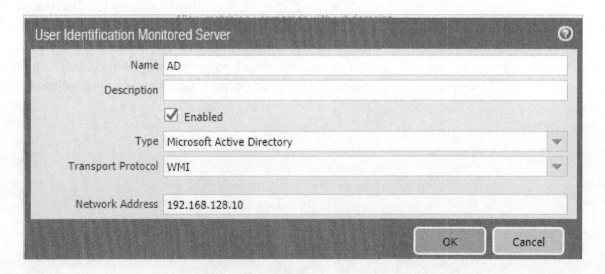

Once the commit completes, if you entered all information correctly, you should see the Status listed as "Connected" under the Server Monitoring section.

	Name	Enabled	Type	Network Address	Status
	AD	✓	Microsoft Active Directory	192.168.128.10	Connected

Server Monitoring

Now, SSH to the CLI of your Palo firewall, then once logged in, enter the command "show user ip-user-mapping all".

```
jbworley79@PA-220> show user ip-user-mapping all

IP                              Vsys              From    User
Timeout(s)
-------------------------------------------------   ---------------------  -------  --------------------
-----------
192.168.168.2                   vsys1             AD      lab\service.account
4
192.168.128.40                  vsys1             AD      lab\domain.admin
5
Total: 2 users
```

As you can see, the firewall has successfully pulled the security logs from AD to form an IP-user-mapping database. If we look in the traffic log, we will now see the "source user" field populated, provided we search for one of the specific IPs mapped to a user.

	(addr.src eq 192.168.168.2)								
	Receive Time	De...	URL Category	Source User	To Port	From Zone	To Zone	Source
	07/30 17:52:31	no	any	lab\service.account	49885	Inside	Farm	192.168.168.2
	07/30 17:52:30	no	any	lab\service.account	135	Inside	Farm	192.168.168.2

As you can see, per the IP-user-mapping database, 192.168.168.2 lists Source User "lab\service.account".

For a test, I will add this user to a security policy using the IP EDL to block traffic to 192.168.128.40. This user, "lab\service.account" is mapped to 192.168.168.2, which is my Palo firewall management interface.

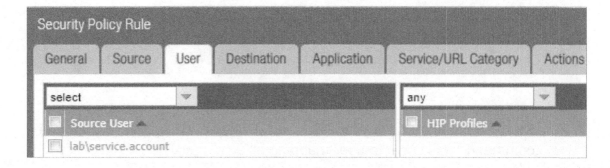

Now, I will return to the Palo CLI, and I will attempt to ping this IP address.

```
jbworley79@PA-220> ping host 192.168.128.40
PING 192.168.128.40 (192.168.128.40) 56(84) bytes of data.
```

I get no response. If I check the Palo traffic logs for "(app eq ping) and (user.src eq 'lab\service.account') and (addr.dst in 192.168.128.40)", I will see that this traffic is blocked per the "IP_Block" rule.

(app eq ping) and (user.src eq 'lab\service.account') and (addr.dst eq 192.168.128.40)

Source User	To Port	From Zone	To Zone	Source	Destination	Action	Rule
lab\service.account	0	Inside	Farm	192.168.168.2	192.168.128.40	deny	IP_Block
lab\service.account	0	Inside	Farm	192.168.168.2	192.168.128.40	deny	IP_Block

Just to confirm, I will initiate a ping from one of my clients to 192.168.128.40.

```
C:\Users\west>ping 192.168.128.40

Pinging 192.168.128.40 with 32 bytes of data:
Reply from 192.168.128.40: bytes=32 time=1ms TTL=125
Reply from 192.168.128.40: bytes=32 time=1ms TTL=125
Reply from 192.168.128.40: bytes=32 time=1ms TTL=125
Reply from 192.168.128.40: bytes=32 time=1ms TTL=125
```

As you can see, this client, sourcing from the same zone as my Palo management interface, successfully receives the echo reply from 192.168.128.40.

						(app eq ping) and (addr src in 192.168.2.10) and (addr dst eq 192.168.128.40)		
URL Category	Source User	To Port	From Zone	To Zone	Source	Destination		Action
any		0	Inside	Farm	192.168.2.10	192.168.128.40		allow

Something is interesting here. My client, 192.168.2.10, is computer lab\west1. I am logged in as west@lab.com, but my user mapping is not there. Why? This is because the firewall did not receive the security log information for my client/username, most likely because it has been hours since my client authenticated with AD. Entering the "show user ip-user-mapping all" command in the CLI of the firewall does not show any entry for 192.168.2.10 or lab\west. I can, however, trigger a security event by locking and unlocking my client computer to force a log entry in AD that will populate the Palo IP-user-mapping database.

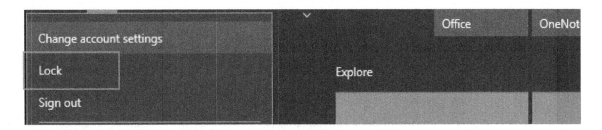

```
jbworley79@PA-220> show user ip-user-mapping ip 192.168.2.10

IP address:      192.168.2.10 (vsys1)
User:            lab\west
From:            AD
Idle Timeout:    2636s
Max. TTL:        2636s
HIP Query:       Disabled
Group(s):        lab\west(1)
```

And now we have it. 192.168.2.10 lists user "lab\west". This is another way to enter the CLI command to look for a specific IP "show user ip-user-mapping ip x.x.x.x". You can also enter a pipe "|" and add a condition "match", followed by a specific string to match "show user ip-user-mapping all | match west".

```
jbworley79@PA-220> show user ip-user-mapping all | match west
192.168.2.10                              vsys1          AD      lab\west
```

Alright, now we need to remove the Palo user agent configuration and switch to the stand-alone user agent we configured on the Windows server. To do this, simply select the Device tab at the top of the browser page and click on the User Identification link in the left-hand column. Then, under the Server Monitoring section, check the box next to your configured AD server, and then click Delete.

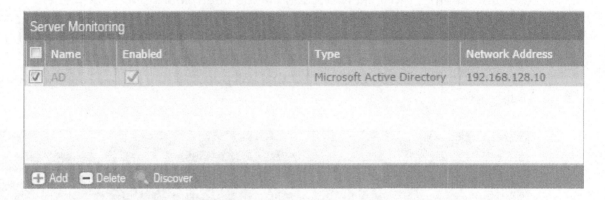

Additionally, under the "Palo Alto Network User-ID Agent Setup" section, click the gear to open the configuration box. Then, remove all the settings, click OK, and lastly commit the config.

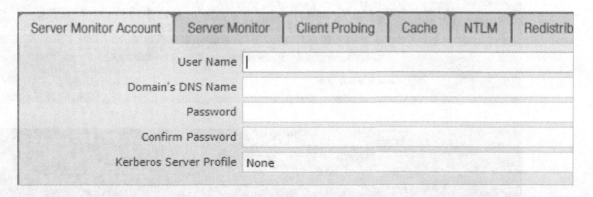

Once the commit completes, under the Device tab, User Identification section, select the "User-ID Agents" tab, then click Add to open the configuration box. Give the User-ID Agent a name (any name). For the "Add an Agent Using" section, select the radio button for "Host and Port", then input the hostname or IP for the agent, and input port 5007 (this is the default setting for the user agent software, but you can change it). Make sure the "Enabled" box is checked, then click OK and commit the config.

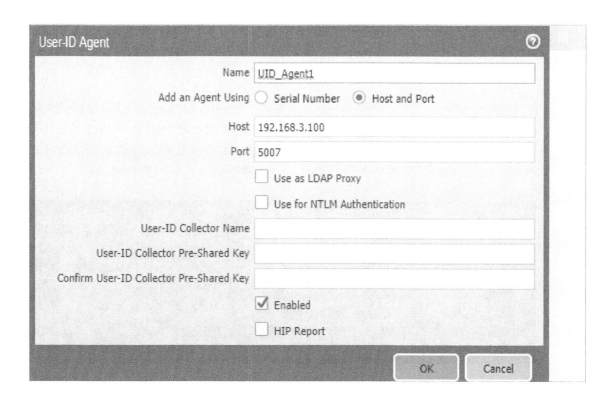

NOTE: After configuring a User-ID Agent, the connected status light will be yellow. It will not establish a connection and turn green until you commit the config.

Once the commit completes, you should see the Connected status as green.

Name	Enabled	Host	Port	Connected
UID_Agent1	✓	192.168.3.100	5007	○

If you return to the Palo firewall CLI and enter the "show user ip-user-mapping all" command, you should see the mapping database populated.

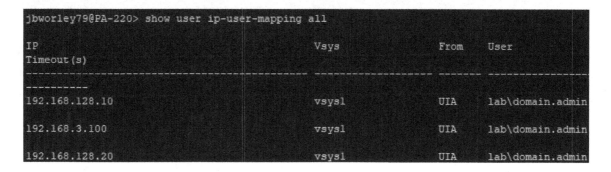

```
jbworley79@PA-220> show user ip-user-mapping all

IP                                          Vsys         From    User
Timeout(s)
---------------------------------------- -------------------- ------- ----------------
----------
192.168.128.10                              vsys1        UIA     lab\domain.admin

192.168.3.100                               vsys1        UIA     lab\domain.admin

192.168.128.20                              vsys1        UIA     lab\domain.admin
```

Notice that the "From" column shows "UIA" versus the previous built-in Palo agent that listed "AD". This just tells you that the information came from a User-ID Agent.

A useful command for checking user agent status is "show user user-id-agent state all". As you can see below, the firewall is connected to 192.168.3.100:5007 and the Status is "conn:idle", meaning it has an established connection but is not actively pulling logs at the moment. The main point: it's connected.

```
jbworley79@PA-220> show user user-id-agent state all

Agent: UID_Agent1(vsys: vsys1) Host: 192.168.3.100(192.168.3.100):5007
        Status                                        : conn:idle
        Version                                       : 0x5
        num of connection tried                       : 1
        num of connection succeeded                   : 1
        num of connection failed                      : 0
        num of status msgs rcvd                       : 61
        num of request of status msgs sent            : 61
```

Another very useful command is "show user user-id-agent config name #AGENT_NAME#". This will tell you the specific configuration of the agent, which is very useful if you do not have the authorization to log into the hosting server. The config output is large, so the figure below is a truncated example.

```
jbworley79@PA-220> show user user-id-agent config name UID_Agent1

OS: Microsoft  (build 9200), 64-bit
Product Version: 8.0.11
Protocol Version: 5

Agent Config:
<?xml version="1.0" encoding="UTF-8"?>
<user-id-agent-config>
<general-settings>
<authentication username="service.account@lab.com" dnsdomain="lab.com" netbiosdoma
<server-monitor security-log-enabled="1" security-log-interval="1" session-enabled
```

Alright, so we know that the firewall is successfully connecting to the User-ID Agent, and it is doing so over TCP-5007. What is this traffic? What does it look like? Well, I took a packet capture of it to show you.

I first disabled the user agent in the Palo, started a packet capture in my lab network, and fired the agent back up. What did I see?

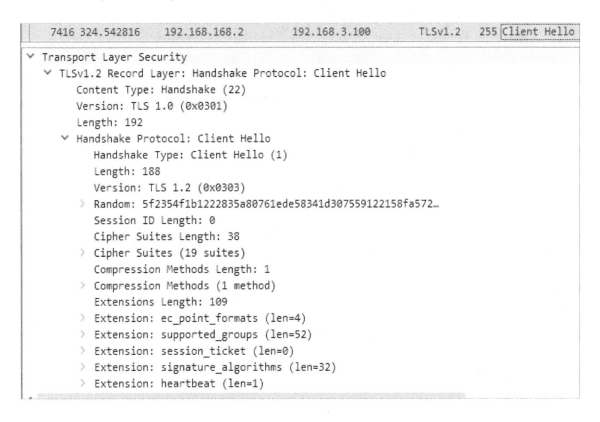

No.	Time	Source	Destination	Protocol	Length	Info
652	136.230298	192.168.3.100	192.168.168.2	TCP	70	[TCP Retransmission
7413	324.541838	192.168.168.2	192.168.3.100	TCP	78	48221 → 5007 [SYN]
7414	324.542360	192.168.3.100	192.168.168.2	TCP	70	5007 → 48221 [SYN,
7415	324.542425	192.168.168.2	192.168.3.100	TCP	64	48221 → 5007 [ACK]

To begin, there is an initial TCP handshake between my firewall (192.168.168.2) and the user agent (192.168.3.100). After the handshake completes, the session moves on to a TLS handshake. Looks like this traffic is going to be encrypted, but I found the negotiation interesting, so I'm including it.

As you can see in the client hello packet below, it does not include any server name extension. It appears similar in context to Internet Explorer, in that it offers 19 cipher suites and includes the heartbeat extension, and it varies in size and uses a length field to identify the total byte count. Chromium-based browsers use 401 bytes for extension headers, and if they don't use all the space, they pad with zeros up to 401 bytes.

7416	324.542816	192.168.168.2	192.168.3.100	TLSv1.2	255	Client Hello

```
˅ Transport Layer Security
  ˅ TLSv1.2 Record Layer: Handshake Protocol: Client Hello
       Content Type: Handshake (22)
       Version: TLS 1.0 (0x0301)
       Length: 192
     ˅ Handshake Protocol: Client Hello
          Handshake Type: Client Hello (1)
          Length: 188
          Version: TLS 1.2 (0x0303)
       > Random: 5f2354f1b1222835a80761ede58341d307559122158fa572...
          Session ID Length: 0
          Cipher Suites Length: 38
       > Cipher Suites (19 suites)
          Compression Methods Length: 1
       > Compression Methods (1 method)
          Extensions Length: 109
       > Extension: ec_point_formats (len=4)
       > Extension: supported_groups (len=52)
       > Extension: session_ticket (len=0)
       > Extension: signature_algorithms (len=32)
       > Extension: heartbeat (len=1)
```

Next, the server (user agent) responds with the server hello, and it provides a certificate. The certificate common name is "User-ID Agent". That's interesting, I didn't configure that, so it must be built into the application.

```
  7417 324.545531      192.168.3.100          192.168.168.2           TLSv1.2  1178 Server He
      v rdnSequence: 6 items (id-at-commonName=User-ID Agent,id-at-organizationalUnitName=
         > RDNSequence item: 1 item (id-at-countryName=US)
         > RDNSequence item: 1 item (id-at-stateOrProvinceName=California)
         > RDNSequence item: 1 item (id-at-localityName=Santa Clara)
         > RDNSequence item: 1 item (id-at-organizationName=Palo Alto Networks)
         > RDNSequence item: 1 item (id-at-organizationalUnitName=Engineering)
         > RDNSequence item: 1 item (id-at-commonName=User-ID Agent)
```

Additionally, this cert is valid from Nov 21, 2014, until Nov 18, 2024.

```
  7417 324.545531      192.168.3.100          192.168.168.2           TLSv1.2  1178 Serv
              v validity
                 v notBefore: utcTime (0)
                       utcTime: 14-11-21 18:50:33 (UTC)
                 v notAfter: utcTime (0)
                       utcTime: 24-11-18 18:50:33 (UTC)
```

Additionally, the server is requesting a client certificate, so we need to make sure there is no "break and inspect" going on with this flow.

```
  7417 324.545531      192.168.3.100          192.168.168.2           TLSv1.2  1178 Server F
         v Handshake Protocol: Certificate Request
              Handshake Type: Certificate Request (13)
```

The client, my Palo firewall, responds with a certificate listing the common name of "Palo Alto Networks Device 410". Is this exclusive to my device? I don't know.

```
7419 324.588112      192.168.168.2        192.168.3.100        TLSv1.2   1518 Cer
```

```
                       ❯ subject: rdnSequence (0)
                         ❯ rdnSequence: 3 items (id-at-commonName=Palo Alto Networks De
                           ❯ RDNSequence item: 1 item (id-at-countryName=US)
                             ❯ RelativeDistinguishedName item (id-at-countryName=US)
                                 Id: 2.5.4.6 (id-at-countryName)
                                 CountryName: US
                           ❯ RDNSequence item: 1 item (id-at-organizationName=Palo Alt
                             ❯ RelativeDistinguishedName item (id-at-organizationName
                                 Id: 2.5.4.10 (id-at-organizationName)
                               ❯ DirectoryString: printableString (1)
                                   printableString: Palo Alto Networks
                           ❯ RDNSequence item: 1 item (id-at-commonName=Palo Alto Netw
                             ❯ RelativeDistinguishedName item (id-at-commonName=Palo
                                 Id: 2.5.4.3 (id-at-commonName)
                               ❯ DirectoryString: printableString (1)
                                   printableString: Palo Alto Networks Device 410
```

Lastly, the validity date for my Palo client cert is Nov 5, 2015, through Jan 1, 2026. Very interesting.

```
7419 324.588112      192.168.168.2        192.168.3.100        TLSv1.2   1518 Cer
```

```
                     ❯ validity
                       ❯ notBefore: utcTime (0)
                           utcTime: 15-11-05 21:20:26 (UTC)
                       ❯ notAfter: utcTime (0)
                           utcTime: 26-01-01 21:20:26 (UTC)
                     ❯ subject: rdnSequence (0)
```

After the TLS negotiation, all traffic is encrypted, so we're not going to see it. That's alright, we know the IP-user-mapping info is being passed inside, so we're good to go.

Now that we're back up and running with a user ID agent, let's test "lab\service.account" again and see if the firewall blocks traffic from this account based on the configured security policy.

Source User	To Port	From Zone	To Zone	Source	Destination	Action	Rule
lab\domain.admin	0	Inside	Farm	192.168.3.100	192.168.128.40	allow	Inside_Farm
lab\service.account	0	Inside	Farm	192.168.3.100	192.168.128.40	deny	IP_Block

Ah, this is interesting. So, initially, the user ID agent was reporting that "lab\service.account" was mapped to 192.168.3.100, but then there was a shift and the user ID agent began to report that "lab\domain.admin" was mapped to 192.168.3.100. I noticed the mapping, and since "domain.admin" was the user logged into the server, I locked and unlocked the server to trigger an update. You see, 192.168.3.100 is the user ID agent server, and since we've configured the agent to use "service.account" to pull the EVENTLOG file from AD, when it does and authenticates with AD, the agent software picks up the new ip-user-mapping. If I look at the agent "Monitoring" link again, I'm sure it will now be back to "service.account".

	service.account	
VM Information Sources		
Monitoring		
Logs	IP Address	User
Server Certificate		
MDM Integration	192.168.3.100	lab\service.account

It is now mapped to "service.account". So, remember, if you have some automated processes running on a platform and using a service account, there is a good possibility that the service account will continuously override the true user. In that case, depending on how your security policies are structured, you might block legitimate traffic, or you could end up giving the user access to resources he or she normally cannot access.

OK, we have one more topic to cover to bring the UserID experience full circle: LDAP Server Profiles.

Section 7.3: Configuring an LDAP Server Profile

Now that we have a working user ID agent, and the firewall can query IP-user-mapping data, we need to be able to add security groups to rules. As I'm sure you'd agree, adding every username to a rule is beyond tedious. If the firewall can perform LDAP lookups, it can take the username information it has cached, and it can query a domain-joined LDAP server to find out in which security groups the username is assigned. Then, per a security policy, the firewall administrator can add the security group containing many users, to allow or deny access to a specific resource. Let's configure this feature and see it in action.

First, select the Device tab at the top, then in the left-hand column, click on and expand the Server Profiles section, then lastly click on the LDAP link. Next, click Add. Once the configuration box opens, give the profile a name, in the "Server List" section, add the details for your LDAP server (in my case, I'm going to use my AD server). Then, under the "Server Settings" section, set "Type" to "active-directory" and add the base DN (for me, the base DN is "DC=lab,DC=com". Next, for "Bind DN", enter your service account in UPN format, enter the password twice, and if using TCP-636 LDAP over SSL, check the box for "Require SSL/TLS secured connection". Once finished, click OK and commit the config.

Now, we need to associate the LDAP Server Profile with our UserID configuration. Select the User Identification link in the left-hand column, then select the Group Mapping Settings tab in the main page area. Next, click Add, and once the configuration box opens, give the Group Mapping a Name, select the LDAP Server Profile, you previously created, under the "Server Profile" dropdown box, then select the "Group Include List" tab at the top of the configuration box.

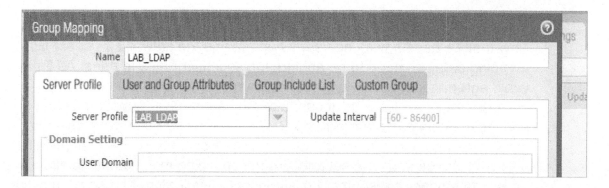

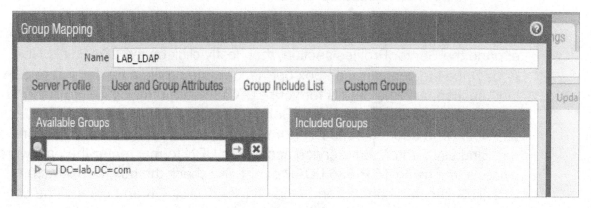

As you can see in the last example, under "Available Groups", I have "DC=lab,DC=com". This is a great way to test your LDAP Server Profile. If you click the arrow next to your available group, and it expands to show the various groups residing on your LDAP server, you know you have successfully configured LDAP for the firewall.

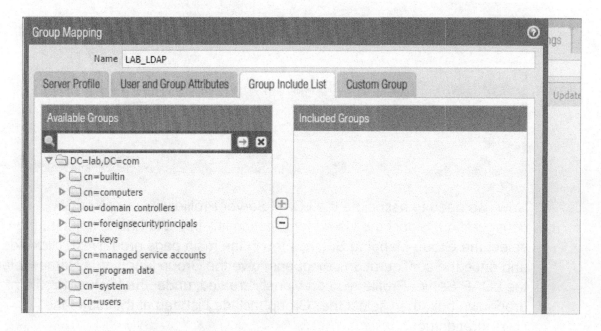

Once you've confirmed that the LDAP Server Profile is working, click OK and commit the config.

NOTE: You can also verify the LDAP profile by accessing the firewall CLI and entering the command string "show users group list". You should see many groups listed, even with a base AD install.

```
jbworley79@PA-220> show user group list

cn=performance monitor users,cn=builtin,dc=lab,dc=com
cn=schema admins,cn=users,dc=lab,dc=com
cn=remote management users,cn=builtin,dc=lab,dc=com
cn=protected users,cn=users,dc=lab,dc=com
cn=access control assistance operators,cn=builtin,dc=lab,dc=com
cn=server operators,cn=builtin,dc=lab,dc=com
cn=network configuration operators,cn=builtin,dc=lab,dc=com
cn=domain controllers,cn=users,dc=lab,dc=com
cn=remote desktop users,cn=builtin,dc=lab,dc=com
```

As a test, I will create a new security group called "Svc Accts" in AD. Then, I will add user "service.account" to this group.

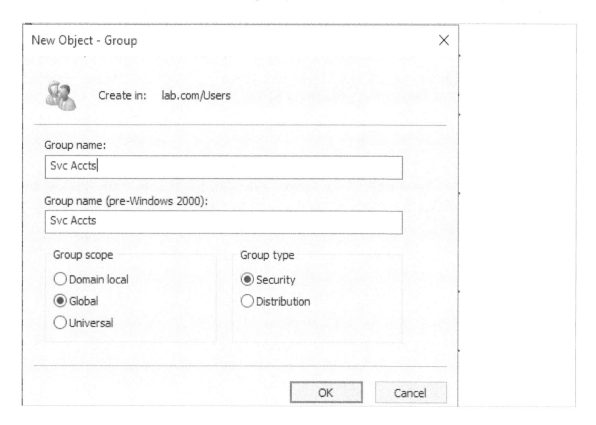

Now, I will return to the Palo, and under the "IP_Block" security policy, I will replace "lab\service.account" with "lab\svc accts".

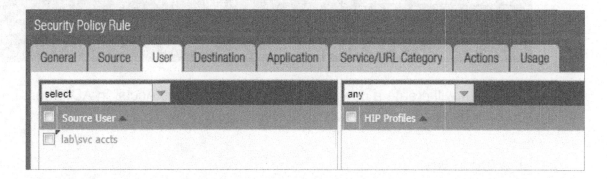

If I try to ping 192.168.128.40 from 192.168.3.100 with the IP-user-mapping set to "lab\service.account", I should be blocked again.

Alright, so we have UserID configured and fully functional. Now, I will show you some useful CLI commands you can use to identify users, groups, and group membership.

Section 7.4: UserID CLI Informational Commands

One of my favorite things about UserID is that it gives me access into AD for various queries without actually having the authorization to log into AD. If I want to know what groups exist in AD, I can enter "show user group-mapping state #LDAP_SERVER_PROFILE#". In my case, my server profile name is "LAB_LDAP".

```
jbworley79@PA-220> show user group-mapping state LAB_LDAP


Group Mapping((null), type: active-directory): LAB_LDAP
        Bind DN    : service.account@lab.com
        Base       : DC=lab,DC=com
        Group Filter: (None)
        User Filter: (None)
        Servers    : configured 1 servers
                ad.lab.com(636)
                        Last Action Time: 811 secs ago(took 0 secs)
                        Next Action Time: In 2789 secs
        Number of Groups: 50
        cn=rds endpoint servers,cn=builtin,dc=lab,dc=com
        cn=terminal server license servers,cn=builtin,dc=lab,dc=com
        cn=distributed com users,cn=builtin,dc=lab,dc=com
        cn=protected users,cn=users,dc=lab,dc=com
        cn=group policy creator owners,cn=users,dc=lab,dc=com
```

If I want to see the list of users associated with a particular group, I can enter the command "show user groups name '#DISTINGUISHED_NAME#'".

```
jbworley79@PA-220> show user group name 'cn=svc accts,cn=users,dc=lab,dc=com'

short name:  lab\svc accts

source type: ldap
source:       LAB_LDAP

[1      ] lab\service.account

jbworley79@PA-220>
```

In the example above, to query the group I created earlier "Svc Accts", I need to enter it as "cn=svc accts,cn=users,dc=lab,dc=com".

NOTE: If you click on a security policy containing a user security group, and you hover the mouse pointer over the group name in the security policy config window, it will show you the string you need to enter, with quotations (single or double) surrounding the entire string.

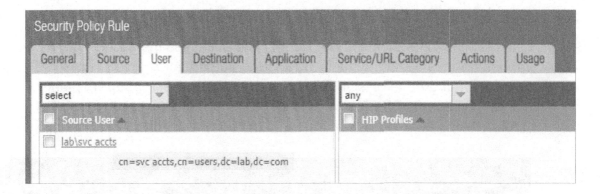

This is called a distinguished name. The common names are "svc accts" and "users". I built the "svc accts" group under the "users" group. Lastly, the string is completed by adding the domain components "lab" and "com". As you can see, the "service.account" is the only user assigned to this group.

```
jbworley79@PA-220> show user group name 'cn=svc accts,cn=users,dc=lab,dc=com'

short name:  lab\svc accts

source type: ldap
source:      LAB_LDAP

[1      ] lab\service.account

jbworley79@PA-220>
```

This command is extremely useful. If you configure an "allowed" security policy with a specific security group that a systems administrator configured, and the user still reports that they cannot access the resource, you can query the group to see if the user was added.

Another useful command is "show user IP-user-mapping". This will show you what is cached in the IP-user-mapping database on the firewall. I covered this previously, but for the organization of this book, I want to add it here to include the "Informational Commands" section. If I'm trying to find a specific user, I can add a literal match for a portion of the user's name. In this case, I will search for the IP-user-mapping for "service.account" by typing in "show user ip-user-mapping all | match service".

The last command I'd like to share is the "show user user-ids match-user" command. This is another very helpful command in the search for traffic associated with a specific user. Say you get a trouble ticket for a blocked website. Usually, this will include some information about the user, but I guarantee it won't list the user's actual username, so you need a way to find it. Say the user is Service Account. You know a fragment of the user's name, but you don't know the exact syntax of the AD username. In this case, I will enter the command "show user user-ids match-user service".

```
jbworley79@PA-220> show user user-ids match-user service

User Name                        Vsys    Groups
---------------------------------------------------------------------
lab\service.account              vsys1                                cn=denied rodc password
com
                                                                      cn=domain admins,cn=users
                                                                      cn=administrators,cn=buil
                                                                      cn=svc accts,cn=users,dc=

Total: 12
*  : Custom Group

jbworley79@PA-220>
```

Based on the fragment "service", the query returned "service.account". Even better, it lists all group memberships for this user.

So, as you can see, UserID is a very powerful feature. By maintaining an IP-user-mapping database, the firewall can track users dynamically. Also, if you configure an LDAP profile to query your LDAP or directory services server, you enable the firewall to use the database to query and match users with specific groups, enabling a much more scalable approach to matching user data within policies. Additionally, UserID gives you the means to gain access to information you might not usually have access to view, such as finding specific usernames based on limited information, or checking to see which groups are available and what users are assigned to those groups. It's very powerful.

Chapter 8: Custom Signatures

I am ending this book with my most favorite subject: custom signatures. I've spent countless hours working to perfect this craft, and what a craft it is. The tedious nature of creating a signature, committing, testing, discovering it doesn't match, changing, committing, over and over again: it will test your patience, but once you get it, it's like a new beginning.

The overarching category for this subject is AppID (application identification). This is the engine that the Palo firewall uses to match and categorize data-rate traffic according to the contents of the application layer in the flow. This process uses pre-defined signatures: either stock AppIDs from Palo, or custom AppIDs you create yourself. In creating custom signatures, you begin by defining the next-layer protocol after IP. Generally, TCP and UDP are considered layer4 protocols, whereas most other protocols are considered layer3. If you're creating a signature to match on a layer3 protocol (ICMP, EIGRP, OSPF), your only option will be to identify the protocol number in the signature. There are no contexts for matching information contained within these protocols when creating custom signatures. I do not know what Palo Alto Networks uses to match these protocols in their stock AppIDs, but it would be really neat to find out.

Also, you might see application layers sitting on top of one another from time to time. For instance, it is common to see NetBIOS over TCP/IP (NBT) and server message block (SMB) in the same packet. In the history of Microsoft computer communications, NBT was primarily used as a name resolution protocol. Network Basic Input Output System (NetBIOS) protocol was originally developed by IBM, and it was meant to only traverse a single subnet/LAN segment. To use it over multiple network hops, Microsoft had to create a new iteration: NBT. However, Microsoft moved to direct hosting long ago, which enabled SMB to operate using DNS; but, if you look at a packet capture of SMB traffic, you will always see a small NetBIOS header before the SMB header.

```
   148 2020-08-09 11:22:05.103142 192.168.2.10      192.168.128.30    TCP    66 51471 → 4
   149 2020-08-09 11:22:05.103840 192.168.128.30    192.168.2.10      TCP    66 445 → 514
   150 2020-08-09 11:22:05.103957 192.168.2.10      192.168.128.30    TCP    54 51471 → 4
   151 2020-08-09 11:22:05.104030 192.168.2.10      192.168.128.30    SMB    127 Negotiate
> Frame 151: 127 bytes on wire (1016 bits), 127 bytes captured (1016 bits) on interface \Device\NPF_
> Ethernet II, Src: VMware_1f:6e:90 (00:0c:29:1f:6e:90), Dst: Cisco_92:96:42 (fc:fb:fb:92:96:42)
> Internet Protocol Version 4, Src: 192.168.2.10, Dst: 192.168.128.30
> Transmission Control Protocol, Src Port: 51471, Dst Port: 445, Seq: 1, Ack: 1, Len: 73
∨ NetBIOS Session Service
     Message Type: Session message (0x00)
     Length: 69
> SMB (Server Message Block Protocol)
```

In the example above, I performed an SMB connection from my client (192.168.2.10) to the server (192.168.128.30). After the TCP handshake completes, the flow transitions to SMB. In the Packet Details window, you can see the NetBIOS Session Service header, followed by the SMB header. According to Microsoft (https://support.microsoft.com/sr-latn-me/help/204279/direct-hosting-of-smb-over-tcp-ip), "Direct hosted "NetBIOS-less" SMB traffic uses port 445 (TCP and UDP). In this situation, a four-byte header precedes the SMB traffic. The first byte of this header is always 0x00, and the next three bytes are the length of the remaining data".

When creating signatures, you have two options concerning syntax: use ASCII, or use Hexadecimal. In both cases, you can incorporate regular expressions. I'm not going to cover regular expressions in this book, but if you're curious, Palo Alto Networks provides a list of regex options you can use in the Palo firewall (https://docs.paloaltonetworks.com/pan-os/8-1/pan-os-web-interface-help/objects/objects-custom-objects/objects-custom-objects-data-patterns/syntax-for-regular-expression-data-patterns). When using hexadecimal, you must identify the start of the hex string with "\x". Then, you must close the hex string with…you guessed it, "\x".

Another major factor for signatures is the requirement set forth by Palo Alto Networks regarding the minimum and maximum characters allowed in a single signature. Your signatures can only contain up to 127 characters, and you must have at least 7 bytes of contiguous static data in the signature without any use of regular expressions. So, you must plan accordingly, especially when deciding on either hexadecimal or ASCII. Hexadecimal requires "\x" twice in the string, which counts against your total character count. Also, every byte in hexadecimal requires two characters, whereas ASCII only requires one.

Now, the first thing I want to cover, for creating custom signatures, is the decryption of Wireshark TLS captures. The vast majority of user traffic is HTTP, which is also tunneled inside of HTTPS. HTTP, with the help of other embedded protocols, is capable of transferring so many types of information. We can transfer files, send/receive emails, send instant messages, watch videos, and so forth. So, to produce a signature that has any value whatsoever, you need to have a way to decrypt the flow and see the secured HTTP traffic inside. Don't get me wrong, you can create signatures based on the initial TLS handshake traffic, in which case it is possible to identify the source browser type, tunneled protocol, and server name indication. But, to have all options complete, you need to see the decrypted traffic too.

Section 8.1: Decrypt TLS Packet Captures

Decrypting packet captures in WireShark, using a Windows PC and a Chromium-based browser is incredibly easy to do. First, from the start menu, type in "this pc". Once the "This PC" App (used to be "My Computer") shows up as the best match, right-click it, and select "Properties".

Then, under Properties, select the "Advanced system settings" link in the left-hand column (enter Administrator credentials, domain, or local, if needed). Once the "System Properties configuration box opens, select the "Environmental Variables…" button at the bottom. Once the "Environment Variables" configuration box opens, under the "System variables" section, click the "New" button. Once the "New System Variable" configuration box opens, enter "SSLKEYLOGFILE" in the "Variable name" field. Next, click on the "Browse Directory" button and decide on a location where you want your session key file to be stored. In my case, I keep it on the desktop. Give the file a name (I used SSLKEYS.txt), then click OK for each configuration box to close everything out.

NOTE: If the user account you want to run Wireshark with is different from the administrator account you used to configure this setting, make sure you browse the directory from C:\Users and select the proper user. In the case above, I used my "domain.admin" account to elevate privileges and configure this environmental variable, and so my initial "Desktop" directory was listed or "domain.admin". As you can see in the example above, I added the full path to the user "west" Desktop directory, which is the Desktop directory for my current user.

Next, open Chrome. The moment it opens, you'll see a new .txt file on your Desktop (or wherever you chose to save the file). In my case, my file name is "SSLKEYS.txt".

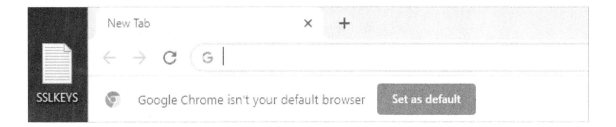

Now, what is inside of this new .txt file? Well, it looks like this.

This file contains the symmetric keys used after asymmetric authentication completes. Per (https://lekensteyn.nl/files/wireshark-tls-debugging-sharkfest19us.pdf), if using TLS 1.2, you will only see the "CLIENT_RANDOM" string. If using TLS 1.3, you'll also see "CLIENT/SERVER_HANDSHAKE_TRAFFIC_SECRET", "CLIENT/SERVER_TRAFFIC_SECRET", "CLIENT RANDOM", and "EXPORTER_SECRET".

Alright, now, open Wireshark, type in "CTRL+SHIFT+p" to open "Preferences". Then, click on and expand the "Protocols" category from the left-hand column, and type in "tls". This should bring you to the TLS protocol configuration. Next, under the "(Pre)-Master-Secret log filename" field, click the "Browse" button and locate the .txt file you created by opening Chrome, select it, and then click the "Open" button. Once you're back on the TLS preferences page, click the OK button.

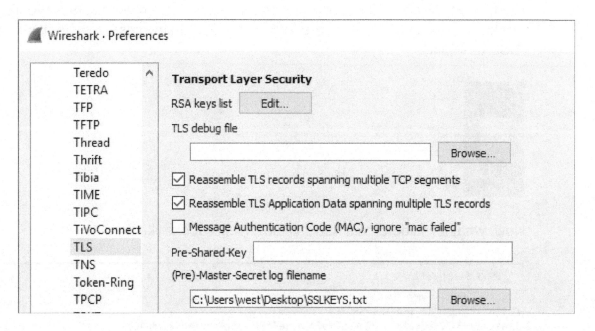

Now, to capture a TLS flow and decrypt it in Wireshark, you need to have Wireshark running first before you browse to a URL. This is because you need to capture the TLS handshake onward so that Wireshark can reference the randoms in the flows to apply the proper secrets. So, let's see how Wireshark looks now. I will start a capture and browse to https://httpvshttps.com. In Wireshark, I will use the filter string (tls.handshake.extensions_server_name contains "httpvshttps").

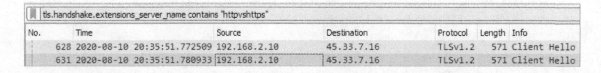

I will look further into the second client hello. If I press "CTRL+ALT+SHIFT+t", it will open the entire TCP flow associated with that client hello. If I look past the TLS handshake, I find an HTTP2 GET request for the root of "httpvshttps.com".

```
642 2020-08-10 20:35:51.854670 192.168.2.10          45.33.7.16          HTTP2    466 HEADERS[1]: GET /
  > Header: :authority: httpvshttps.com
  > Header: :scheme: https
  > Header: :path: /
```

If I continue down into the flow, I will also see find a 301, permanently-moved response from the server. In the case of HTTP2, this is located in the HEADERS section.

```
653 2020-08-1…  45.33.7.16   192.168.2.10          HTTP2    208 SETTINGS[0], WINDOW_UPD
  > Header: :status: 301 Moved Permanently
  > Header: date: Tue, 11 Aug 2020 00:36:09 GMT
  > Header: content-type: text/html
  > Header: content-length: 166
  > Header: location: https://www.httpvshttps.com/
```

If I scroll down a bit further, I will find the GET request for www.httpvshttps.com without a request to negotiate a new TLS connection.

```
657 2020-08-1…  192.168.2.…  45.33.7.16          HTTP2    127 HEADERS[3]: GET /
  > Header: :method: GET
  > Header: :authority: www.httpvshttps.com
  > Header: :scheme: https
  > Header: :path: /
```

So, you can see the benefit of decrypting the flow to analyze the HTTP1.1/HTTP2 flow. If I had not decrypted, I would not have known that a 301 redirect had taken place. Alright, now that we have Wireshark decrypting, let's make our first signature.

Section 8.2: A Case Study - Matching User login for Dropbox

STOP! First, make sure you are decrypting flows in the firewall before you attempt to make any signatures on traffic contained within a TLS tunnel. In our case, we will be matching on HTTP1.1/HTTP2.

Why am I making a signature to match on a Dropbox username? Because it's interesting, of course! First, I will start Wireshark, then I'll browse to https://www.dropbox.com. Once the page loads, I'll check the server certificate to make sure it's signed by my Palo decrypt cert.

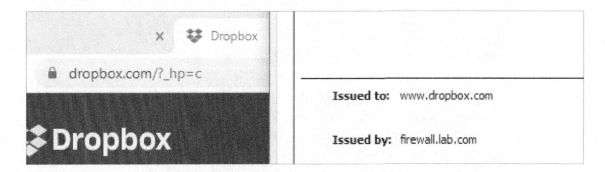

And it's decrypted. Good deal. Now, I will log in with username usaf.telephony.guy@gmail.com.

Great, I'm in. Next, I will close out the browser and focus my attention on Wireshark. Since I know that I'm decrypting TLS, I will not focus on searching for the server name indication. Instead, I will do general HTTP/HTTP2 searches for "usaf". This is unique enough that it should provide some data.

No.	Time	Source	Destination	Protocol	Length	Info
3740	2020-08-10 21:32:34.580634	192.168.2.…	162.125.6.1	HTTP2	166	DATA[173]
3744	2020-08-10 21:32:34.611855	192.168.2.…	162.125.6.1	HTTP2	167	DATA[175]
3910	2020-08-10 21:32:46.358386	192.168.2.…	162.125.6.1	HTTP2	1195	DATA[181]
3951	2020-08-10 21:32:48.056131	192.168.2.…	162.125.6.1	HTTP2	203	DATA[183]
4022	2020-08-10 21:32:52.164781	192.168.2.…	162.125.6.1	HTTP2	205	DATA[185]
4028	2020-08-10 21:32:52.182113	192.168.2.…	162.125.6.1	HTTP2	1568	DATA[189]

> Form item: "login_email" = "usaf.telephony.guy@gmail.com"

So, the ASCII string "usaf" is contained within URL-encoded form packets. If I look at the raw data, I will see the result of the URL encoding.

```
6c 6f 67 69 6e 5f 65 6d   61 69 6c 3d 75 73 61 66    login_em ail=usaf
2e 74 65 6c 65 70 68 6f   6e 79 2e 67 75 79 25 34    .telepho ny.guy%4
30 67 6d 61 69 6c 2e 63   6f 6d 26 63 6f 6e 74 3d    0gmail.c om&cont=
```

Ok, so the "@" symbol in the email was converted to URL encoding with the string "%40". What does this mean? Well, if you look up hexadecimal code 0x40 in an ASCII table, you will find an "@" symbol. So, this raises the question: what will the firewall match on? Will it be a URL encoded match "usaf\.telephony\.guy%40gmail\.com", or should we revert the "@" to hexadecimal and use "usaf\.telephone\.guy\x40\xgmail\.com"? We'll try both: naming one signature "DROPBOX_USAF_URL_ENCODE" and one signature "DROPBOX_USAF_HEX".

To start, I will select the final packet with the string "login_email=usaf.telephony.guy%40gmail.com", and I will right-click and select "Follow / TCP Stream". Once the TCP stream filter loads, you'll notice the packet directly above the URL-encoded packet is an HTTP POST action to "/ajax_login".

| 3909 | 2020-08-10 21:32:46.358250 | 192.168.2.… | 162.125.6.1 | HTTP2 | 137 | HEADERS[181]: POST /ajax_login |
| 3910 | 2020-08-10 21:32:46.358386 | 192.168.2.… | 162.125.6.1 | HTTP2 | 1195 | DATA[181] (application/x-www-f… |

⌐ HTML Form URL Encoded: application/x-www-form-urlencoded

I am going to use this as part of my signature. If I drill down into this POST packet, I find the Authority www.dropbox.com. I can match this. Also, if I look at "path", I see "/ajax_login".

> Header: :authority: www.dropbox.com
> Header: :scheme: https
> Header: :path: /ajax_login

So, what about the URL-encoded form packet? I have an HTTP host match www.dropbox.com, an HTTP path match "/ajax_login", so what is the context for a URL-encoded form? Let's look at the printable text.

```
is_xhr=true&t=VrgCSIxeVo2Zbv2EZ_OjGOVL&login_email=usaf.telephony.guy%40gmail.com&cont=
%2F&remember_me=true&g-recaptcha-response-v3=03AGdBq25jjLUfd2Z5-
7AokKeisq_GgAB2Lcd0PwNqj0qj9mxbCkxrweV9iWkr0wJEq7GrMt2Mn-
0c4KNyfW3TkiHpGz3CX4rlsP9CClN3VxM6Wmwk00nW_MiFCTmyzklgI4k0-
xF87r9Ij_BYpGQ7y8BC3ZhEjw74KbO_lNMpllz3qhVqv5N45Hi-
Jszvtxb85HI5twHQhJGDA92WkVBnpvSs37nBS_wHeVATWBGAVeeLp-7Uimwr66DDjR1_MvpGPs_Kdk6e-LqV-
uIdUbPGELXrC6Z-nyFK3dpJ2px4iO9gVaAUzy451qDvl3FJ4SgfNu80BFbiydFDCh1KY5JAtMt5zL4O-
```

At first glance, this looks like parameter information, meaning that the URL would contain a "?" to denote the start of a query, and this URL-encoded form data would follow. There are several conditions separated by an ampersand "&". Take a look at a www.google.com search for palo alto networks. If you observe the resulting URL string from the search, you'll see a similar data syntax: https://www.google.com/search?rlz=1C1VFKB_enUS660US660&ei=Fv4yX6rpM K6sytMP0dS3gA8&q=palo+alto+networks&oq=palo+alto+networks&gs_lcp=CgZ wc3ktYWIQAzILCC4QxwEQrwEQkwIyAggAMgIIADICCAAyAggAMgIIADICCAAy AggAMgIIADICCAA6BwgAELADEEM6DQguEMcBEK8BEAoQkwI6BAgAEApQqq T1Y0Upg- VZoAXAAeACAAVuIAZ0CkgEBNJgBAKABAaoBB2d3cy13aXrAAQE&sclient=ps y-ab&ved=0ahUKEwiqzN2s_ZPrAhUulnIEHVHqDfAQ4dUDCAw&uact=5

In the above example, the authority is www.google.com, the path is "search", and the parameter is everything after the "?". If you contrast the parameter string in this search with our capture of the URL-encoded form data from www.dropbox.com, I'm sure you'll agree it looks very similar.

Also, when it comes to application signatures, you need to check and see what application is currently assigned to the flow. Why is this? Well, Palo has possibly created a stock application to match this traffic, and their match is most likely the best. In general, if the traffic is classified by Palo as SSL or web-browsing, you're fine to create your signature and have it match without any issues 99.9% of the time. However, if Palo has taken the step of creating a specific AppID for the traffic, you'll have a hard time creating a better match than Palo. Instead, it is best to find out what AppID Palo has assigned, then assign this AppID as the "parent app" when creating the custom AppID. That way, you're not in competition. In the case of our dropbox traffic, I ran a check using the URL Filtering logs and applying a URL Filtering Log filter (url contains "www.dropbox.com/ajax_login").

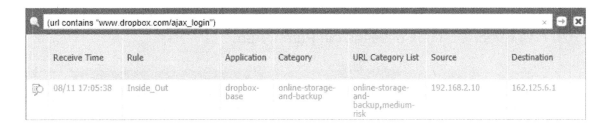

	Receive Time	Rule	Application	Category	URL Category List	Source	Destination
	08/11 17:05:38	Inside_Out	dropbox-base	online-storage-and-backup	online-storage-and-backup,medium-risk	192.168.2.10	162.125.6.1

As you can see, the application is listed as "dropbox-base", so I'll use that as the parent app.

Alright, to test how the Palo will pick up on URL-encoded "@", I'll make two signatures: one using the URL code for "@", which is "%40", and I'll make another using the hexadecimal value for "@", "0x40".

Signature 1:
Name: DROPBOX_USAF_URL_ENCODE
Port: tcp/443
       Context 1: http-req-host-header
              Signature 1: "www\.dropbox\.com"
       Context 2: http-req-uri-path
              Signature 2: "/ajax_login"
       Context 3: http-req-params
              Signature 3: ".*login_email=usaf\.telephony\.guy%40gmail\.com.*"

Signature 2:
Name: DROPBOX_USAF_HEX
Port: tcp/443
       Context 1: http-req-host-header
              Signature 1: "www\.dropbox\.com"
       Context 2: http-req-uri-path
              Signature 2: "/ajax_login"
       Context 3: http-req-params
              Signature 3: ".*login_email=usaf\.telephony\.guy\x40\xgmail\.com.*"

First, I will create the signature "DROPBOX_USAF_URL_ENCODE". To do this, select the Objects tab at the top, then in the left-hand column, select the Applications link, and lastly click Add. Once the application configuration page opens, give the custom application a name, then under the "Properties" section, select the "Category", "Subcategory", and "Technology" identification information using the dropdown menus. For my configuration, I'm choosing the first item that shows up for these dropdown boxes since these values are required, but I do not necessarily care what these values list at this point. With that said, you should make it a habit to input information that properly identifies the application. Lastly, I'll select "dropbox-base" as the Parent App.

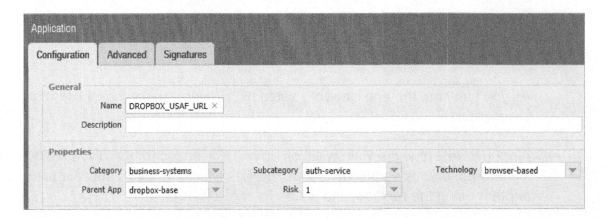

Next, on the Advanced tab, I will select the "Port" radio button under the Defaults section. Then, I will click Add and input the protocol/port. In this case, I'm using TCP-443, so I will input it as "tcp/443". If you get confused on the syntax, just look below the Defaults section. There is a legend on how to enter the data.

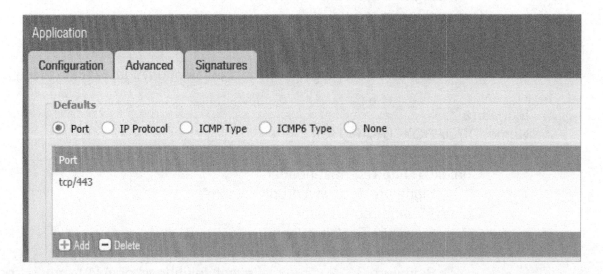

Now, I will select the Signatures tab. To begin, you must select Add, then you'll be presented with the Signature configuration box. First, I will give it a name (in my case, "URL"), select the "Session" radio button, make sure the "Ordered Condition Match" box is checked.

Then, I will click "Add or Condition" at the bottom of the configuration box. When you make your first signature, you can click either "Add Or Condition" or "Add And Condition". There is no existing signature entry to "And/Or" with. However, when you make additional signature entries, you need to be mindful of which one you choose. If you want all entries to match, then you "And" them. If you want to choose between two options, you "Or" them. In my case, I will "And" all entries, meaning all of them will need to match. Also, with the "Ordered Condition Match" box checked, they must present in the flow in the order in which I add them (And Condition 1, And Condition 2, …). When the "Condition" configuration box opens, I will select Operator as "Pattern Match", then under context, I will first select "http-req-host-header". Lastly, under the Pattern field, I will input "www\.dropbox\.com". Then, I will click OK.

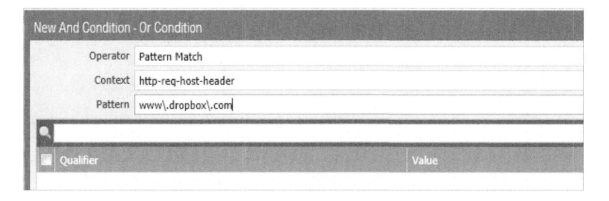

Now, I still have two other contexts to add, but instead of walking through them, I will present my main signature page showing the configuration. You'll notice that I added the signatures just as I listed them previously in this chapter. Also, for the other AppID (DROPBOX_USAF_HEX), all configuration will be the same, except for the signature name and configuration for context "http-req-params" (URL is using "%40", HEX is using "\x40\x").

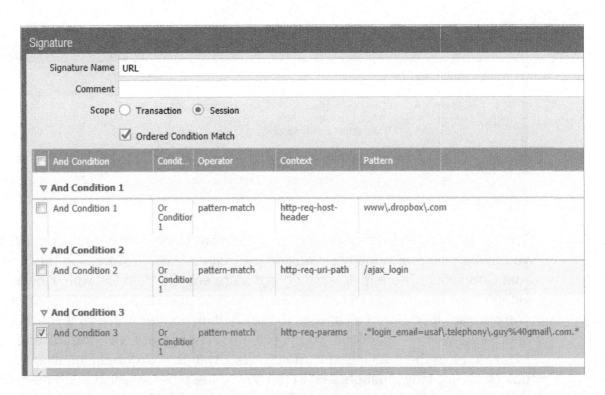

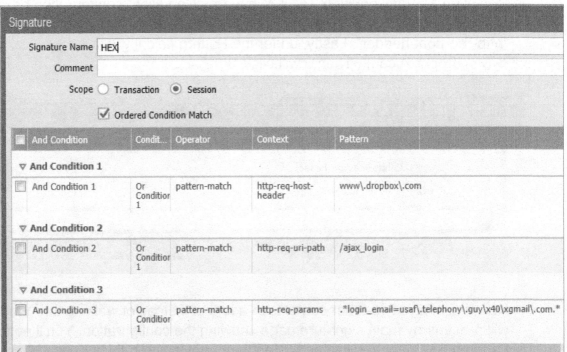

Now, all that's left to do is close out the config boxes and commit the config.

NOTE: When you make a new signature, of any kind, and you commit, it will take quite a bit longer to complete. I have read that this is due to the Palo firewall recompiling the signature database.

Now, I will return to the traffic log, input a filter, set the refresh rate to 10 seconds, browse to and log into www.dropbox.com, and we'll see which AppID wins. I have walked you through the process to pull up the traffic log, so I won't needlessly repeat the process. For my filter, I will use "((rule eq DROPBOX_USAF_URL_ENCODE) or (rule eq DROPBOX_USAF_HEX)). This filter will show any traffic that gets classified as either one of these AppIDs.

Looks like hexadecimal wins. This is an interesting behavior, in that Wireshark shows the raw data displayed as "%40", even accounting for the binary/hex values of each character, but the flow is sending a literal ASCII "@". Just be aware of these types of differences between the captures and what is matched. One method I've used in the past to find a working context and/or variation in strings is to make an AppID with the same signature applied to multiple "OR" contexts, or multiple OR contexts of the same type with the variations in signatures. Then, I would generate traffic, check for a match, remove a signature, commit, and try again. If you continue this until the traffic no longer matches, you know you just removed the working context/signature combination.

Ok, so we have a match. Let's see if we can block this and keep usaf.telephony.guy@gmail.com from logging in. To do this, I will apply this signature to my "Block_Apps" rule.

Now that my config has finished committing, I will attempt to log into www.dropbox.com with username usaf.telephony.guy@gmail.com, and I'll run filter (app eq DROPBOX_USAF_HEX) in the traffic log to see what the firewall does. As I browse to and attempt to log into www.dropbox.com, I have developer tools running in Chrome. Each time I click "Sign in", the POST error at the bottom of the dev console increments with a "503 – Service Unavailable" error.

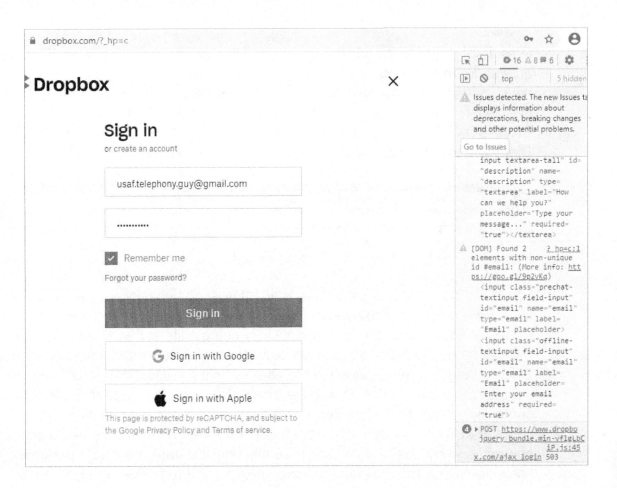

If I look at the Palo traffic log, I see why. This traffic is being blocked, as it should be.

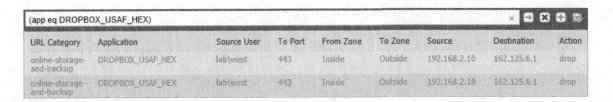

URL Category	Application	Source User	To Port	From Zone	To Zone	Source	Destination	Action
online-storage-and-backup	DROPBOX_USAF_HEX	lab\west	443	Inside	Outside	192.168.2.10	162.125.6.1	drop
online-storage-and-backup	DROPBOX_USAF_HEX	lab\west	443	Inside	Outside	192.168.2.10	162.125.6.1	drop

If I try a different user, I will log in without any issue.

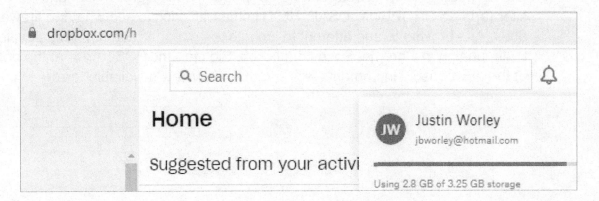

So, as you can see, you can get very granular with signatures. In this case study, I was able to match on a username (email address) to allow or deny logins. In most situations, you would probably want to create a general block rule for www.dropbox.com/ajax_login using a custom URL category or URL EDL, stick it in a deny rule, create a new AppID using OR operations for multiple usernames in the HTTP parameter context, and assign it to an allow rule above the URL deny rule. Another thing to consider is blocking traffic for www.dropbox.com authentication using Google and Apple. You would need to analyze the traffic using these logon methods to find a match via URL or application signature that you could use to deny traffic per security policy.

Section 8.3: A Case Study - Matching SMB File Requests

SMB traffic is a bit unusual, in that directory and file names come down the wire in ASCII format, but each character is separated by 1-byte hexadecimal value 0x00. You would think that if you wanted to match on and block access to \\fileserver\private_lists, you could simply input this string and call it a day. Not so. Let's look at some SMB traffic. I will connect to my EDL server at \\web.lab.com\edl\domain.txt and copy the "domain.txt" EDL to my desktop. Notice that I'm using lower case "domain.txt".

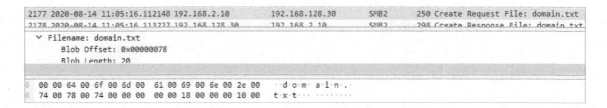

So, looking at the "Create Request File" packet, it does list "domain.txt", however, if you look at the raw data in the hexadecimal field, you'll see each character separated by 0x00. When you make a signature for this type of traffic, you must include the 0x00 hexadecimal value interlaced with the ASCII characters. Ok, so we have a way forward to solve that issue. What about case sensitivity? Except for base64 strings and such, browsers convert URL strings to lower case, but what about SMB? I will attempt to connect to the file share using all caps for the file name "DOMAIN.txt". If SMB changes the flow to lower case, I should see lower case letters in the packet capture.

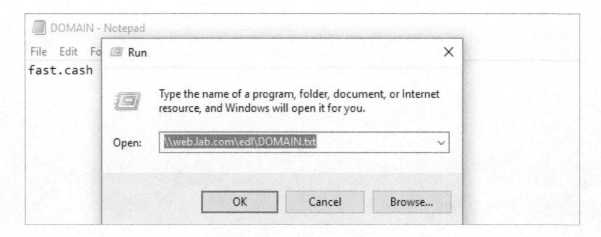

Let's see what happened in the packet capture.

	Time	Source	Destination	Protocol	Length	Info
smb2.filename						
	11 5.832017	192.168.2.10	192.168.128.30	SMB2	250	Create Request File: DOMAIN.txt

It did not change to lower case. What does this mean for our signature? Well, ASCII "D" and "d" are two different values, so our signature will need to account for both, and we'll need to follow this logic for all letters Dd, Oo, Mm, Aa, Ii, Nn. This can get complicated. For instance, consider that I have a total of 6 characters in the name "domain". Each character has two possible values. Sound familiar? This is a binary structure, and since I have 6 binary decisions, I have a total of 64 possible combinations...WOW! Remember, I need 7 bytes of contiguous data, so any hope of "[Dd][Oo][Mm][Aa][Ii][Nn]" is off the table. Also, the Palo will exhibit strange behavior if I enter a string, such as "d\x00\xo\x00\xm\x00\xa\x00\xi\x00\xn\x00\x" and I try to follow up with any condition using regex, such as "\.(txt|txT|tXt|Txt...)". The Palo will error out saying that I must have 7 continuous bytes of data. Well, I do, I just interlaced hex with ASCII, but it is a solid "more than" 7 bytes. So, to fix this, I will have to convert all ASCII characters to hex and input the entire string in hex format...WOW!

Ok, so we need to break down this problem. I have 6 characters, but I certainly do not want to input 64 signatures. Maybe I can strike a happy medium. If I begin the signature with any variation of "doma", I can slim it down to 16 OR signatures. Now, for the remaining characters "in", I can create a regex OR condition for the four iterations "in", "iN", "In", "IN". If I convert everything to hex and interlace the 0x00s, it will look like this.

```
domain_to_hex - Notepad                                              —    □

File  Edit  Format  View  Help
ASCII                       HEX
----------------            --------------------------------------
doma(in|iN|In|IN) -         \x64006f006d006100\x(\x69006e\x|\x69004e\x|\x49006e\x|\x49004e\x)
domA(in|iN|In|IN) -         \x64006f006d004100\x(\x69006e\x|\x69004e\x|\x49006e\x|\x49004e\x)
doMa(in|iN|In|IN) -         \x64006f004d006100\x(\x69006e\x|\x69004e\x|\x49006e\x|\x49004e\x)
doMA(in|iN|In|IN) -         \x64006f004d004100\x(\x69006e\x|\x69004e\x|\x49006e\x|\x49004e\x)
dOma(in|iN|In|IN) -         \x64004f006d006100\x(\x69006e\x|\x69004e\x|\x49006e\x|\x49004e\x)
dOmA(in|iN|In|IN) -         \x64004f006d004100\x(\x69006e\x|\x69004e\x|\x49006e\x|\x49004e\x)
dOMa(in|iN|In|IN) -         \x64004f004d006100\x(\x69006e\x|\x69004e\x|\x49006e\x|\x49004e\x)
dOMA(in|iN|In|IN) -         \x64004f004d004100\x(\x69006e\x|\x69004e\x|\x49006e\x|\x49004e\x)
Doma(in|iN|In|IN) -         \x44006f006d006100\x(\x69006e\x|\x69004e\x|\x49006e\x|\x49004e\x)
DomA(in|iN|In|IN) -         \x44006f006d004100\x(\x69006e\x|\x69004e\x|\x49006e\x|\x49004e\x)
DoMa(in|iN|In|IN) -         \x44006f004d006100\x(\x69006e\x|\x69004e\x|\x49006e\x|\x49004e\x)
DoMA(in|iN|In|IN) -         \x44006f004d004100\x(\x69006e\x|\x69004e\x|\x49006e\x|\x49004e\x)
DOma(in|iN|In|IN) -         \x44004f006d006100\x(\x69006e\x|\x69004e\x|\x49006e\x|\x49004e\x)
DOmA(in|iN|In|IN) -         \x44004f006d004100\x(\x69006e\x|\x69004e\x|\x49006e\x|\x49004e\x)
DOMa(in|iN|In|IN) -         \x44004f004d006100\x(\x69006e\x|\x69004e\x|\x49006e\x|\x49004e\x)
DOMA(in|iN|In|IN) -         \x44004f004d004100\x(\x69006e\x|\x69004e\x|\x49006e\x|\x49004e\x)
```

Now that's complex, and it's certainly prone to human error. In reality, if you're looking to match on SMB, you're much better off matching on the path for a specific directory, which you could ensure is named with 3-4 letters, or even better: include 7 digits in the name and call it a day.

Ok, let's see how this works with an AppID. I'm not going to walk the process again since it is nearly identical to the process used for the www.dropbox.com AppID. This signature will be formulated using these parameters:

Name: EDL_SMB
Port: tcp/445
Context: "ms-ds-smb-req-v2-create-filename"
Multiple OR'd Signatures for "domain": **NOTE:** See example above

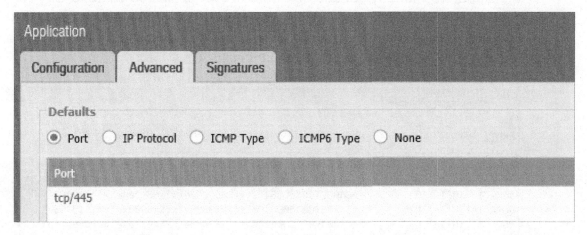

Observing the signatures below, you can see there is 1 And Condition "And Condition 1", and being that I scrolled to the bottom, there are 16 Or conditions for that single And condition. With this signature, the firewall will run the entire list until it finds a match. Now, I will wrap this up by closing out the configuration and performing a commit.

Next, I will attempt to connect to the file share using a varied combination of upper and lower case for the file name "DoMaIn.txt". At the same time, I will perform a packet capture for the SMB file name. Lastly, I will check the traffic log for the appropriate AppID classification.

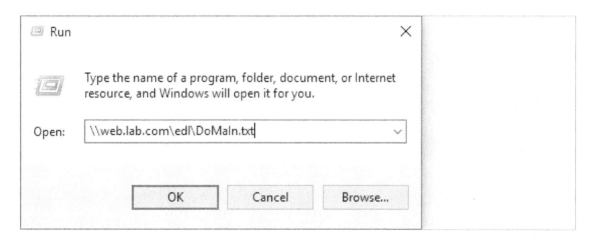

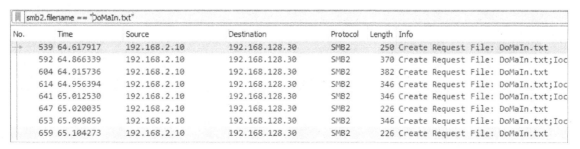

(addr.src in 192.168.2.10) and (addr.dst in 192.168.128.30) and (port.dst eq 445)							
Application	Source User	To Port	From Zone	To Zone	Source	Destination	Action
EDL_SMB	lab\domain....	445	Inside	Farm	192.168.2.10	192.168.128.30	allow

As you can see, the name transferred as "DoMaIn.txt", and the firewall correctly classified it as the custom AppID "EDL_SMB".

Custom AppIDs can be extremely powerful, especially for organizations with unique requirements. Again, it can be a very tedious and cumbersome process, but if you take the time to thoroughly analyze the packet captures and ensure your signature syntax is free of error, you will be pleasantly surprised with the results.

This concludes all topics of this book. The Palo Alto Networks Next-Generation Firewall is a fantastic creation. What this box can do, coupled with the speed at which it does it, is truly amazing. With that said, any technology, no matter how robust, must be explored to fully understand the capabilities. Taking on such a task and growing through the process makes one a much better administrator and engineer.

I hope you enjoyed the journey, and I also hope you use the information provided as a building block for your continued testing and experimentation with this amazing platform. Thank you.

Made in the USA
Las Vegas, NV
29 December 2024

15529484R00103